ISBN: 9781290538114

Published by:
HardPress Publishing
8345 NW 66TH ST #2561
MIAMI FL 33166-2626

Email: info@hardpress.net
Web: http://www.hardpress.net

MESSRS. LONGMANS & CO.'S NEW LIST

A NEW LENT BOOK
With an Introduction by the BISHOP OF LONDON

SPIRITUAL PROGRESS: A Word of Good Cheer. By the Rev. ARTHUR W. ROBINSON, D.D., Vicar of All Hallows, Barking by the Tower. Crown 8vo, 2s. 6d. net.

THE REASON OF LIFE. By WILLIAM PORCHER DU BOSE, M.A., Author of "The Gospel in the Gospels," &c. Crown 8vo, 5s. net.

This is an attempt to present the Christian creed, as a whole, as the completely adequate expression of the meaning and value of life.

STRENGTH FROM QUIETNESS: Suggestions for Keeping a Quiet Day, chiefly addressed to Invalids, and those unable to join in a Retreat. Including Addresses by Bishop KING and Dean BUTLER. By M. GILES. Fcap. 8vo, 2s. net.

THE CHURCH AND THE AGE. Being Four Lectures delivered at Sion College on "The Co-operation of the Church with the Spirit of the Age." By the Very Rev. WILLIAM RALPH INGE, D.D., Dean of St. Paul's. Fcap. 8vo, 2s. net.

LOVE'S ASCENT: Considerations of Some Degrees of Spiritual Attainment. By the Rev. JESSE BRETT, L.Th., Chaplain of All Saints' Hospital, Eastbourne. With Frontispiece in colour. Crown 8vo, 3s. 6d. net.

THE PASSION OF CHRIST. A Study in the Narratives, the Circumstances, and some of the Doctrines pertaining to the Trial and Death of our Divine Redeemer. By the Rev. JAMES S. STONE, D.D., Rector of St. James's Church, Chicago. Crown 8vo, 4s. 6d. net.

SERMONS AND ADDRESSES DELIVERED IN THE DIOCESE OF LONDON. By FREDERIC EDWARD RIDGEWAY, D.D., Bishop of Salisbury. Crown 8vo, 5s. net.

MARRIAGE WITH A DECEASED WIFE'S SISTER. By the Rev. F. W. PULLER, M.A., of the Society of St. John the Evangelist Crown 8vo, 3s. 6d. net.

A SHORT INTRODUCTION TO THE OLD TESTAMENT. By the Rev. F. ERNEST SPENCER, M.A. Crown 8vo, 2s. 6d. net.

OUR BOUNDEN DUTY: Sermons and Addresses. By the Rev. CHARLES H. ROBINSON, D.D., Hon. Canon of Ripon, and Editorial Secretary of the S.P.G. Crown 8vo, 2s. 6d. net.

A DEVOTIONAL PSALTER. By the Rev. CHARLES H. ROBINSON, D.D. Fcap. 8vo, cloth 1s. net; leather 2s. net.

LONGMANS, GREEN AND CO.
LONDON, NEW YORK, BOMBAY, AND CALCUTTA

MESSRS. LONGMANS & CO.'S NEW LIST

SERMONS AND ADDRESSES. By EDWARD KING, D.D., late Bishop of Lincoln. Edited by B. W. RANDOLPH, D.D., Canon of Ely. Crown 8vo, 2s. 6d. net.

LIFE AND WORK OF THE REV. T. T. CARTER, Hon. Canon of Christ Church, Oxford, and Warden of the House of Mercy, Clewer. By J. F. M. CARTER. Based on "The Life and Letters of Thomas Thellusson Carter," by Archdeacon Hutchings. With 5 Illustrations. Crown 8vo, 3s. 6d. net.

PAIN AND GLADNESS: A Biblical Study. By a SISTER in an English Community. With a Preface by the Rev. JOHN NEVILLE FIGGIS, Litt.D. Crown 8vo, 2s. 6d. net.

CONFESSION IN THE CHURCH OF ENGLAND SINCE THE REFORMATION: A Paper read at Cambridge, Lent, 1911. By B. W. RANDOLPH, D.D., Canon of Ely. Crown 8vo, 1s. net.

CREED AND THE CREEDS: Their Function in Religion. Being the Bampton Lectures for 1911. By the Rev. JOHN HUNTLEY SKRINE, M.A., Vicar of St. Peter's in the East, Oxford. 8vo, 7s. 6d. net.

STUDIES IN THE RESURRECTION OF CHRIST. An Argument. By the Rev. CHARLES H. ROBINSON, D.D., Hon. Canon of Ripon and Editorial Secretary of the S.P.G. Fcap. 8vo, 2s. 6d. net. Popular Edition, crown 8vo, gilt top, paper covers, 6d. net.

THE RESURRECTION AND MODERN THOUGHT. By the Rev. W. SPARROW SIMPSON, D.D., St. Mary's Hospital, Ilford. 8vo, 15s. net.

IDEALS OF HOLINESS: An Aid to Preparation for Holy Communion. By the Rev. F. W. DRAKE, Priest-in-Charge of St. John's Church, Wilton Road, S.W. Crown 8vo, 2s. net.

THE HOLY EUCHARIST: A Series of Lectures. By the Rev. W. C. E. NEWBOLT, M.A., Canon and Chancellor of St. Paul's Cathedral. Fcap. 8vo, 1s. net.

FATHER POLLOCK AND HIS BROTHER MISSION PRIESTS OF ST. ALBAN'S, BIRMINGHAM. With a Prefatory Letter by the Right Rev. CHARLES GORE, D.D., Bishop of Oxford. Crown 8vo, 2s. 6d. net.

CHOSEN AND SENT FORTH: Notes of a Retreat for Priests. By the Rev. JOHN WAKEFORD, B.D., Prebendary of Clifton in Lincoln Minster. Fcap. 8vo, 2s. net.

STEDFASTLY PURPOSED: Notes of a Retreat for Church-women. By the Rev. JOHN WAKEFORD, B.D., Prebendary of Clifton in Lincoln Minster. Fcap. 8vo, 2s. 6d. net.

LONGMANS, GREEN AND CO.
LONDON, NEW YORK, BOMBAY, AND CALCUTTA

THE CHURCH AND THE AGE

BY THE SAME AUTHOR

PERSONAL IDEALISM AND MYSTICISM. The Paddock Lectures for 1906, delivered at the General Seminary, New York. Crown 8vo, 3s. 6d. net.

SPECULUM ANIMÆ: Four Devotional Addresses given in the Chapel of Corpus Christi College, Cambridge, to Public Schoolmasters and College Tutors. Fcap. 8vo, 1s. 6d. net.

LONGMANS, GREEN AND CO.
LONDON, NEW YORK, BOMBAY
AND CALCUTTA

THE CHURCH AND THE AGE

BY

WILLIAM RALPH INGE, D.D.

DEAN OF ST. PAUL'S
HONORARY FELLOW OF JESUS COLLEGE
CAMBRIDGE

LONGMANS, GREEN AND CO.
39 PATERNOSTER ROW, LONDON
NEW YORK, BOMBAY, AND CALCUTTA
1912

All rights reserved

PREFACE

Though it is not usual for a showman to begin by disparaging his own wares, I feel that some apology is needed for printing addresses which were not written for publication, which were delivered to a very quiet little society of London ladies, and the theme of which was neither chosen by the lecturer nor particularly congenial to him. I am also reluctant even to seem to have been provoked to justify myself against the absurd misrepresentations of the halfpenny newspapers and their reporters. I am printing these addresses not on their account, but in deference to strong requests which I could hardly disregard, from those who heard them and many others. The latter, I fear, will find my remarks less bold and original than they had been led to expect.

I approached my allotted theme with a slight feeling of irritation, as I pictured to myself the kind of treatment of it which was probably expected from me. I have lived long enough to hear the *Zeitgeist* invoked to bless very different theories. When I first began to read books on great subjects, the Spirit of the Age was supposed to be a rationalist in religion, an absolute idealist in philosophy, a materialist and determinist in natural science. Now all these opinions are out of fashion, with the individualism that was often associated with them; and a new set of catchwords has taken their place. Forgotten truths and discarded errors have emerged again, hand in hand, from their hiding-places. So the rhythm of human thought is maintained; the slow pulsation of the racial life goes on.

Now it is not the office of the Church of Christ to be a weathercock, but to witness to the stable, eternal background in front of which these figures cross the stage, and so to preserve and maintain precisely those elements of the truth which are in most danger of being lost. For this reason, it rarely happens that the Church can "co-operate" with a popular movement; more often it is compelled to protest against its onesidedness. If we consider at what periods the Church has been most true to itself, and has conferred the greatest benefits on humanity, we shall find that they have been times when Churchmen have not been afraid to be "in the right with two or three." Like certain ministers of state, the Church has always done well in opposition, and badly in office.

The only possible explanation of this is that Christianity is essentially a struggle for an independent spiritual life. It can mould society from above, as it were, but it can never entangle itself with any human institutions without disastrous results to itself and them. The new birth is admission into the citizenship of a spiritual kingdom; and the citizens of a spiritual kingdom must maintain complete independence in face of all external conditions. The Christian, it has been said, is the Lord's servant, the world's master, and his own man. If this is true, there is much in the prevailing tone and temper of modern thought which is a standing menace to the Christian spirit. "The substance of the spiritual life," says Eucken in one of his latest books,[1] "is threatened by the fact that the omnipotent State is inclined to treat that life, in all its branches, as a mere means towards the attainment of its own particular aims; to look upon science and art, and especially religion and education, with a view to what they achieve for the aims of the State, and to shape them as much as possible in accordance with these aims; there is also a strong tendency to follow the same course to accomplish the ends of the contemporary form of government. An independent and genuine spiritual life can hardly offer too great an opposition to such a perversion, with its deification of human forms. . . . Nothing can save us from sinking to be mere

[1] *Life's Basis and Life's Ideal*, p. 359, 360.

puppets of the soulless mechanism of the State, if we do not find the power to maintain the life of the soul against all attempts of encroachment." This is no imaginary danger. Not long ago I read in a periodical edited by a highly placed ecclesiastic, and an ardent social reformer, the following words over the signature of the editor himself, "To the State, and the State alone, we must look for *salvation.*" And about the same time a prominent socialist said in my hearing to an audience largely composed of clergymen, "The Church is an organ of the State"; and no one but myself cried "No, no," at this impudent Erastianism. A church that was an organ of the State would be useless for any purpose except that of helping the State to crush liberty and silence prophets, a task that has no doubt been congenial to some churchmen.

It is unfortunate that those among us who have a firm grasp of the truth that the Church must be independent of the State are for the most part influenced either by jealousy of the Church of England or by the strangely external and mechanical theory of Catholicity which prevails in High Anglican circles. A church does not necessarily lose its spiritual independence, nor its liberty of opposing the temporal power, because it has a recognised position as an estate of the realm. It is by no means certain that our Church would become more independent after disestablishment, especially if the lax and tolerant control of the Nineteenth Century State were exchanged for subservience to "Catholic tradition," the dead hand of mediæval theory and practice. The living Spirit of Christ is plainly no respecter of persons or of denominations; and it is this living Spirit which must be the guide and teacher of the Church of the future.

I see no reason to retract or apologise for what I have said about democracy, though it will be seen that my remarks on that subject were not intended to take a prominent place in these addresses. Scores of correspondents have congratulated me on my "courage"; but surely we have not yet so far lost our liberty in England that a man may not criticise or even ridicule a popular political theory. I called democracy a superstition and a fetish; and I repeat that it is plainly both. The so-called "will of the people" is merely the whim of the majority. I cannot agree with Lord Morley that "the poorest and most numerous class is the People"; it is simply the poorest and most numerous class. And a political mob has no will; it has only passions and aspirations, which are played upon by astute demagogues, who have studied the psychology of crowds in the manner described by a masterhand more than two thousand years ago. "These mercenary individuals [the Sophists] teach nothing but the opinion of the many, that is to say, the opinions of their assemblies; and this is their wisdom. I might compare them to a man who should study the tempers and desires of a mighty strong beast who is fed by him—he would learn how to approach and handle him, also at what times and from what causes he is dangerous or the reverse, and what is the meaning of his several cries, and by what sounds, when another utters them, he is soothed or infuriated; and you may suppose further, that when, by continually attending upon him, he has become perfect in all this, he calls his knowledge wisdom, and makes of it a system or art, which he proceeds to teach, although he has no real notion of what he means by the principles or passions of which he is speaking, but calls this honourable, and that dishonourable, or good or evil, or just or unjust, all in accordance with the tastes and tempers of the great brute. Good he pronounces to be that in which the beast delights, and evil to be that which he dislikes, and he can give no other account of them except that the 'just' and 'noble' are names which we gave to the necessary?"[1] No imposture so gross as this could maintain itself, if it were not a real superstition. "To dispense equality to equals and unequals is to found the public order on a lie; it is contrary to the elementary principles of human society,

---

[1] Plato, *Republic*, p. 493.

which rests upon the natural fact of inequality of value. . . . At the present time all political power is centred in the hands least fitted to exercise it: wisdom, wealth, culture, experience —all the most vital forces of society—are virtually ostracised."[1] My quarrel with the democratic theory is not that it is revolutionary, but that it is utterly absurd and irrational, and that in practice it brings into power just the kind of men whom we might have expected, *à priori*, that it would favour. In France and the United States, politics is hardly a profession for an honourable man. The national assemblies of these democracies reflect faithfully all that is worst in the national character.

The charge of pessimism that has been brought against me is ridiculous. No Christian can be a pessimist. Christianity is a system of radical optimism, inasmuch as it asserts the ultimate correspondence of value and existence, or, to put the same thing in less technical language, it asserts that all will be well, some day and somehow. But optimism of this kind is a shallow mockery if it does not rest on a drastic revaluation of the goods and evils of human life, and on a firm belief in human immortality. These are both found in Christianity. The Christian doctrine, as I understand it, is that there is an eternal and spiritual state of existence, in which the Divine

[1] W. S. Lilly, *Idola Fori*, pp. 37–8.

attributes of goodness, wisdom, and beauty are fully realised and fully operative. This state of existence we call Heaven. But since the Creator desires that those attributes which are part of His nature should be worked out, according to their capacity, by His creatures, He has caused to exist the world which we know, a world the true meaning and reality of which are to be found in moral purpose, in intellectual activity, and in art. (Religion rightly lays its stress on the first of these, without depreciating the others.) These things have all a timeless value, while almost all else fades and passes. The healthy soul *loves* whatever it sees to possess these values, and recognises its kinship with it. This "love" for God, and for God's image in man and nature, is the unfailing token of spiritual health, and the hierophant of all the higher mysteries of existence. Christianity never puts its hope on temporal *results*, because it rates those results very low, as compared with spiritual values. Nor does it look for a millennium on this earth. The world-order, according to our belief, only exists as an arena in which the good is to actualise itself through conflict. A perfect world would have no more *raison d'être*. Nevertheless, as I have argued, we may reasonably expect great improvements in the constitution of human society and, which is far more important, in human nature. For the human race is an unit in God's sight; an unceasing purpose runs through our history. But the process of improvement will (so far as we can foresee) be so slow as to be hardly perceptible, unless indeed we discover how to breed goodness and ability as race-horses are bred for swiftness and cart-horses for strength. I confess that my hopefulness for the future of civilisation is based on the reasonable expectation that humanity is still only beginning its course. Nor can I see that it is any less agreeable to speculate on a truly rational and happy mode of existence ten thousand years hence, a hope which may be realised, than on a socialistic Utopia about 1950, which will certainly not be realised. The happiness of our remote descendants concerns us as much as that of our grandchildren and great-grandchildren. It is folly, not rational optimism, to forget that "the mills of God grind slowly," repeating the error of those who "thought that the kingdom of God should immediately appear."

But after all, the main argument of my addresses was not that democracy and socialism are undesirable allies because they are based on unsound principles and foster impossible expectations, but that the Church must be faithful to the example and precepts of her Founder, who declared that His kingdom was not of this world. Secularised Christianity has neither savour nor salt. True Christianity is not a religion that will ever be acceptable to the majority ; it is too stern and uncompromising. But an earnest and faithful Church, even if its adherents were in a small minority, would do a great deal indirectly towards social amelioration, by holding up a standard of public opinion which few could venture openly to neglect, and by undermining that strange amalgam of superficial culture and deep-rooted barbarism, of pride and timidity, of shrewdness and ignorance, which the New Testament calls "the World." For the Christian standard of values, so far as it is adopted, demonetises the World's currency, and substitutes another, which has this extraordinary quality, that it has no natural limit of increase, and that what we give to others we also make more truly our own.

CONTENTS

		PAGE
I.	THE SPIRITS OF THE AGE	1
II.	THE SPIRIT OF THE AGES	21
III.	THE CHURCH	43
IV.	WHAT CAN WE DO?	66

THE CHURCH AND THE AGE

I

THE SPIRITS OF THE AGE

YOUR committee have most kindly invited me to give four lectures on "The Co-operation of the Church with the Spirit of the Age." It is a charming subject. It calls up quite an idyllic picture. The Spirit of the Age! A beautiful maiden, alert, strenuous, intellectual, self-confident. Determination is written on her mouth, though some perplexity furrows her brow. She begins to doubt whether she can carry out all her great ideas unaided. When behold, there comes to meet her the Church—a still more beautiful maiden, with a serene and far-away look in her eyes; with even more determination in her mouth, and no perplexity on her brow. Lo! she holds out her hand to her sister, while with the other arm she points to the steep and narrow path which they must henceforth climb side by side. I have tried to conjure up this picture—that is easy; and to bring it into some relation with actuality—that is difficult. When I quit the enchanted realm of abstractions, so full of poetry, so simple and orderly—the land where everything has a name expressing its character, and always behaves as a thing so named ought to behave—the land where things do not overlap and get entangled with each other, still less masquerade in each other's clothes, wolves calling themselves sheep, jays peacocks, and demons angels of light—when I quit this enchanted realm and turn my eyes upon the world of reality, where things are always passing into each other without ceasing to be themselves, where nothing ever stands still to be ticketed, where instead of stable unchanging concepts we have to deal with fluctuating facts and varying values—like the mad croquet match in *Alice in Wonderland*, when the mallets twist into flamingoes and the hoops and balls walk about the lawn—I look about for my beautiful maiden, the Spirit of the Age, but I cannot find her. And the other still more beautiful maiden, where is she? She, surely, cannot be hard to find.

> "We are not divided,
> All one body we,
> One in faith and doctrine,
> One in charity!"

But that is too alarming a topic, not to

be tackled to-day. In my third address, if I have not frightened you all away before that time, I will approach it with fear and trembling. To-day let us examine two of our other terms—"The Age" and its "Spirit." What do we mean by "the Age"? When did it begin? When we were born? When we remembered, or forgot, to change 8 into 9 in writing the second figure Anno Domini? There are no boundary lines in the time process, as Bergson has taught us—no beginnings and no endings. It is our intellect which always tries to chop up time into lengths. It is convenient, but deceptive. We are all very proud of our so-called historical method, which consists essentially of trying to squeeze ideas into the form of time; but they always ooze out. However, we *can* cut off lengths of past time for purposes of comparison, and if we remember what we are doing, there is no reason why we should not. Let us then, obedient to our thesis, compare the twentieth century, as far as it has gone, with the nineteenth. We soon notice that our "age," like every other age, is the rebellious child of its predecessor. The romanticists of the nineteenth century had no patience with the rationalists of the eighteenth. Wordsworth called Voltaire " dull " (we have not got Voltaire's opinion of the Ecclesiastical Sonnets). The last quarter of the nineteenth century scoffed at Tennyson; some of the youngest generation are tired of Browning. We are nearly all undutiful enough to want to put our parents' household gods in the cupboard. Renan, in his detached way, said that one task which lies before the twentieth century is to fish out of the waste-paper basket the various valuable articles which the nineteenth has thrown into it. Well, it may be true that our fathers and grandfathers threw too much into the waste-paper basket; but I will hazard the sweeping statement that the nineteenth was in many ways the most remarkable century since the beginning of history. Among its possible rivals the period which witnessed the discovery of America, the Renaissance and Reformation, Shakespeare and the printing-press, can alone compare with it for massive achievement. At the beginning of the epoch Europe shook off some of the shackles which had bound it for ages. The transition so much admired by Herbert Spencer, "from status to contract," took full effect. There was a vast industrial development, calling into existence dense populations such as the earth had never supported before. The European races established their ascendancy over the whole planet, introducing the blessings of their civilisation to the savage peoples, whom they exterminated, and to the farthest Orientals, who are rapidly learning from us how in the distant future they may perhaps exterminate the Europeans. Such a harvest of scientific discoveries has never been crowded into three generations as the steam-engine, electricity, photography, the telegraph and telephone, spectrum analysis, and the rest. In literary achievement the nineteenth century ranks only just behind the very greatest.

There are, no doubt, deductions to be made. As Houston Chamberlain says, the material element is too predominant. It was essentially a century of *accumulation*. Not ideas, but material gains, are its characteristic feature. Chamberlain even says: " In other respects (besides accumulation) it is neither fish nor flesh ; it wavers between empiricism and spiritualism, between *liberalismus vulgaris* (as it has been wittily called) and the impotent efforts of senile conservatism, between autocracy and anarchism, doctrines of infallibility and stupid materialism, worship of the Jew and anti-Semitism, the rule of the millionaire and proletarian government." An age of ferment, no doubt ; but, in spite of its critics, one of great and almost unique achievement.

Now the great century is over, and civilisation is sitting pensively in the midst of her accumulations, like the figure of Melencolia in Dürer's famous picture. The era of scientific discoveries is happily not yet closed. The last ten or twenty years have brought to light wireless telegraphy, the transformation of chemical elements, and the aeroplane; while great things are hoped for from bacteriology. But in all other fields signs of exhaustion are very apparent. If we were asked to pick out three great men among our own contemporaries—men whom even partial friends and admirers could without absurdity place in the same rank which the verdict of competent judges has granted to at least a dozen of the Victorians, we should find it impossible, I am afraid, to meet the challenge. There is a great deal of second and third-rate ability just now, but a dismal dearth of genius. It may be a case of *reculer pour mieux sauter*: the future alone can decide whether it is so, or whether we are on the down-grade; but for the present we must face the fact that our lot is cast in a rather unpromising and uninspiring time; the race-spirit is resting on its oars after an exhausting spurt. I do not think that this can be seriously disputed.

The results of the great discoveries remain; but the creeds and philosophies based upon them are crumbling. In the mid-Victorian period there was a buoyant confidence that the riddles of the Sphinx had been solved, which we cannot any longer feel. Where is the cocksure complacency of the philosophic radicals, the blatant assurance of the materialistic scientists, the arrogance of Darwin's first disciples, the calm superiority of theological liberalism? The world now seems much more complex and mysterious; the facile solutions which then seemed so obvious now fail to satisfy us. I am far from saying that this scepticism is a sign of degeneracy. It may be a wholesome disillusionment. Only this is plain, that while our grandfathers marched on with head erect and a confidence that victory was theirs, we are conscious of profound contradictions and unsolved problems.

I am not competent to say much about science; but I can see that the same kind of change is coming over such studies as biology, which any student of contemporary thought can trace in philosophy and religion. It is commonly said that the mechanical theory is breaking down, and that "organic" and "vitalistic" views are taking its place. The older assumption was that we can explain the phenomena of life, even of the higher forms of life, by the principles and laws which are found to hold good for inorganic, "dead" matter. This theory was found to lead to a rather depressing materialism and determinism. Man was proclaimed to be "only the cunningest of nature's clocks." Religion and ethics protested against this degradation of humanity; and it now appears that even on purely scientific grounds their protests were well grounded. Natural selection, which some of Darwin's disciples, more confident than their master, believed to be the sufficient cause of evolution, now appears to be only negative in its action. It is a method of eliminating inefficient variations: it does not explain the fact of variation at all. And variation, or mutation, seems to be more drastic and more freakish than any one supposed twenty years ago. More and more converts are made to vitalistic theories resembling those of Lamarck, once supposed to be quite discredited. A growing mass of evidence seems to point to a kind of inner teleology, a self-directing, albeit unconscious, evolution which is much more than a mere unpacking of what was in the box all the time. "*Creative Evolution*" is the title of Bergson's great work, a title chosen as a challenge to the mechanical theory which deprived the time-process of all meaning and value, by representing each stage as containing nothing that was not implicit in the stage next before it. This, we are now told, would be merely pseudo-evolution. Real evolution implies free, self-determined growth; it implies *creation*, not merely unpacking and unfurling. But if this *real* evolution takes place, it means that the laws which govern organic life must be different from those which govern inorganic. "Why seek ye the living among the dead?"

It means that the conduct of living beings cannot be predicted and calculated upon as men work out a mathematical problem; that even if we knew all the forces, we could not, from them, calculate a necessary resultant. Free-will, once almost abandoned as a theoretical truth, though always admitted in practice, is seen to be capable of being defended philosophically. Therewith the uniformity of nature, which the mechanical scientists believed themselves to have established, though it was only a working hypothesis, is seriously threatened. Naturalistic monism is badly shaken. If inorganic nature follows one law, and life another, or if life is a law to itself, where is the unity of nature which has been such a fruitful hypothesis, the foundation indeed of all modern science?

We can trace, I think, the working of this new tendency of scientific and philosophic thought in several other departments. The grip of natural law is relaxed. Indeed, the very idea of natural law has changed. A law of nature, we are now told, is a description of the way in which nature usually behaves—nothing more. If nature chooses every now and then to behave differently, there is nothing on earth to prevent her. Creatures of habit like to have a fling now and then. So we not only see free-will asserting itself against determinism, but even miracles are rehabilitated. The supernaturalist once more confidently urges his own method of bringing together matter and spirit by dovetailing them into each other in the world of phenomena; and the pragmatist, with exultant war-whoops, dances on the prostrate form of absolute idealism, and claims that whatever satisfies human needs is true—truer at any rate than anything which does not, since truth is only a pedantic synonym of usefulness.

But the victories of natural science, won, all of them, under the banner of the uniformity of nature, are too recent, and the confidence in scientific method is too great and too well-grounded, for scepticism to make much headway within the proper frontiers of nature-study. Science pursues her well-tried methods, and the results continue to be satisfactory. And supernaturalism—the theory of occasional interventions—belongs to the psychology of religious belief rather than to strict science or philosophy. It is a bridge to connect the worlds of nature and spirit; it is not a theory which science and philosophy need take much account of as affecting their own researches. The most remarkable product of the undecided conflict between mechanism and vitalism is the sceptical or sophistical theory of knowledge which in philosophy is called *pragmatism*, and which in theology is the basis of *modernism*. Religious activity in this century will be marked, I believe, by the conflict of two schools, the one rationalistic, strongly ethical, and Protestant; the other, half sceptical, half superstitious, frankly adapting itself to "human needs," lower as well as higher, and maintaining a dualistic severance between truths of faith and truths of fact. This *is* modernist Catholicism: it is indeed the way in which Catholicism has fought its campaigns for the most part; but it was extremely *naïve* of the modernist priests to think that they could give away the *arcana imperii* with impunity.

We have found, then, as the first of our "tendencies of the present age," this revolt against mechanical and determinist views of human life. Our generation, as compared with its predecessor, is disposed to believe in free-will and spontaneity. It can give a good account of itself in rejecting the older mechanical theory. But since the real laws, if there are any, which control the higher forms of life are not yet discovered, there is a great deal of wild and chaotic theorising about the relations of mind and matter, and a recrudescence of puerile superstition which almost makes one wish back again the iron hand of Victorian naturalism. We must hope, however, that the extravagancies of this newly found liberty will be pruned away.

These intellectual movements are only recognised by a few, though a thoughtful observer can trace their ramifications almost everywhere. But for the man in the street, the tottering of the great industrial fabric of the nineteenth century dominates all other issues.

Under the old régime of status, competition was never very keen; and at first the new individualistic industrialism seemed only to stimulate a healthy rivalry which got out of each man the best work that was in him. But every system carries within itself the seeds of dissolution. We need not recount again the too familiar tale of how *men*, rather than their tasks, have been subdivided, how work has been dehumanised and despiritualised; how the speeding up of these monotonous processes imposes an intolerable strain on the nerves of the worker; how the conditions of town life have ruined the physique of the labouring class; and lastly, how various causes combine to make us breed from our worst stocks, so that a progressive degeneration is taking place.

To any one who is able to view the situation without prejudice or passion, the outlook is disquieting in the extreme. We amassed a population of 46 millions on two small islands, while Englishmen were making England the workshop of the world. Great Britain has enjoyed certain accidental advantages of which we have made full use. Our position just off the mainland of Europe gave us the advantage in securing the Atlantic trade; we have coal and iron in abundance, and close together; we have had in the past good and cheap labour. Of these advantages some are passing away inevitably, others are being wantonly sacrificed. America is now the natural centre of the world's commerce, because the Pacific is becoming as important a trade route as the Atlantic; we are no longer the most favoured nation geographically. Our coal supply is being exhausted with criminal recklessness. And our labour is no longer very good, and is becoming extremely dear. We cannot long remain the workshop of the world under these changed conditions. As surely as water finds its own level, so surely will the transfer of industries and wealth, first to America and then to Eastern Asia, be the necessary sequel to the European labour movement.

In this country, at any rate, the twentieth century is the spendthrift heir of the nineteenth. The working-man seems to have resolved to make himself comfortable by taxing capital—in plain terms, by looting the accumulations of Queen Victoria's reign, and living on the rates and taxes. He will have, I think, a short life and a merry one, and his children's teeth will be set on edge.

For these reasons I cannot join the chorus of the lay and clerical advocates who, when they tell us to " co-operate with the spirit of the age," really mean that we should co-operate with the labour movement. Socialism, or almost any other experiment, might answer in Australia, till the British fleet ceases to patrol the ring-fence; but in England I fear that the conditions are ideally unfavourable for those who hope to see a dense population with high wages and short hours.

Let us listen to some other popular cries, and see whether they seem more hopeful as a basis of " co-operation."

It is, or ought to be, a commonplace that the very first duty of any one who wants to understand the signs of the times is a critical examination of current shibboleths and catchwords. Mankind is just as prone as ever to create fetishes. The only difference between us and the savage is that he makes an idol of wood or stone, while we dress up some misunderstood idea in fantastic clothes, and worship that. We light a fire and compass ourselves about with sparks, as the Old Testament prophet said, and then we dance round it, invoking the name of our god. It is quite as easy to hypnotise oneself into imbecility by repeating in solemn tones " Progress, Democracy, Corporate Unity," as by the blessed word Mesopotamia, or, like the Indians, by repeating the mystic word " Om " five hundred times in succession.

The catchword *Progress* I shall leave for my

next address. A great deal of nonsense about Progress has been and still is talked; but we are losing faith in it—indeed, I think rather too much. Some of our newest guides deny that any progress—any real progress as distinguished from mere accumulation of experience—can be traced in humanity itself. That seems to me too pessimistic, and not to be borne out by a candid study of history.

Democracy is perhaps the silliest of all fetishes that are seriously worshipped among us. The method of counting heads instead of breaking them is no doubt convenient as a rough and ready test of strength; and government must rest mainly on force. It is also at least arguable that democracy is at present a good instrument for procuring social justice, and for educating citizens in civic duty. But that is really all that any one has a right to say in its favour. To talk to the average Member of Parliament, one might suppose that the ballot-box was a sort of Urim and Thummim for ascertaining the divine will: that the odd man enjoys a plenary inspiration, like the Bishop of Rome when he speaks *ex cathedra*. This superstition is merely our old friend the divine right of kings ("the right divine of kings to govern wrong") standing on its head; and it is even more ridiculous in that posture than in its original attitude. There is absolutely no guarantee in the nature of things that the decision of the majority will be either wise or just; and what is neither wise nor just ought not to be done. This is a somewhat elementary truism to enunciate to an intelligent audience; but there stands the ridiculous fetish, grinning in our faces, and the whole nation burns incense before it. It is, I think, our duty, to challenge any one who talks of the "right" of the majority to do whatever they think fit, as follows: "Your statement implies one of two things. Either you believe that the majority of every political aggregate is divinely inspired with wisdom and justice, which is a gross and absurd superstition; or you assert, with Thrasymachus in Plato's *Republic*, that justice is only a name for the interest of the stronger; a doctrine which the conscience of humanity agrees with Socrates in stigmatising as grossly immoral." After that, you will not need to ask my opinion of the bishop who published a sermon called "The Democratic Christ and His Democratic Creed." It was not thus that our Master brought comfort and strength to the weary and heavy laden.

Corporate unity is another catchword which needs critical examination, but in a more respectful tone. I shall have more to say about this in my third address, when I deal with "The Church." Here I will only say, first, that a corporate whole is constituted by its internal harmony and consistency, not by the rigidity of the spikes which it interposes between itself and those outside. Next, that the comparison of a society to an "organism" is only an analogy, and one that does not correspond very closely with the facts. A human person has far more independence over against society than a hand or foot over against the whole body. Society exists for him as well as he for society; indeed it is an unjustifiable and very misleading personification of an abstraction to speak of the State as having rights and duties apart from the individuals who compose it. Above all, *we belong to a great many social organisms, each with indefeasible but limited claims upon us.* We cannot admit that all other organisms ("organisations" would be a much better word) are, as we are sometimes told, only "organs of the State." The family, for instance, and the Church, are much more than this. The main problem of practical ethics is to adjust the rival claims of the various organisations to which we belong; and, in dealing with this problem, declamations about corporate unity do not help us at all. We have our duties to our family, to our neighbours, to our profession, to our country, to our Church, to the comity of civilised nations, to humanity, perhaps to the whole cosmic process so far as we understand it. We must strenuously resist any claims on the part of any one of those aggregates

B

to enslave or deny the rights of the others. "Honour all men; love the brotherhood; fear God; honour the King."

There are certain other currents of opinion which, though they seem to me more local, more superficial, less likely to continue, than those with which we have been dealing, must not be left out unconsidered. There is the *counter-revolution* provoked by the orgies of 1793, which, in opposition to liberalism of all kinds, created a revival of mediævalism in architecture, art, and religion. History seems to show that revivals are always only stop-gaps. They indicate that existing institutions are not giving satisfaction or doing their work properly; they generally do some good service by " pulling out of the waste-paper basket " some objects of value which have been too hastily thrown into it; they create a sentiment of sympathy with the past; they emphasise the essential identity of human needs at different periods; but as revivals they have their day, and pass. The past can never be reconstructed; history never repeats itself—it only resembles itself.

In ethics we have a well-marked *humanitarian* movement, and a violent revolt against it, in the philosophy of Nietzsche. On one side, this humanitarian movement marks a real progress, which we may hope will be permanent. The brutal and stupid cruelties which were allowed to disfigure our civilisation till the last century now fill us with amazement. But there is a soft and flabby side to modern humanitarianism which is the result of a long peace and industrial activity. The horror of taking life under any circumstances seems to me unnatural, and probably only temporary. The State of the future, I believe, will kill mercifully but freely.

Another temporary current which is already losing its force is that of *nationality*, patriotism, or imperialism. It draws its power from a blend of noble and ignoble sentiments. We call it noble patriotism in ourselves, and brutal aggressiveness when it is displayed by the Germans. It is a sentiment which is perhaps falling out of touch with facts, since the European nations have a common civilisation, and the classes in each nation have much more in common with the same class in other countries than with other classes in their own. So it is plain that international combinations, in the interests of capital, labour, the Church, learning, research, &c., are taking, and in the future will more and more take, the place of geographical divisions. If men were reasonable beings this ought to bring to an end the monstrous waste of our resources upon armaments.

Well, "the spirits of the age" do not come very gloriously out of our scrutiny. My next address will be more cheerful in tone, for I do believe in the progress of humanity, though I believe it is painfully slow, and that it advances in spirals, "with many a backward-streaming curve." We happen to be living at the end of a very great and remarkable period, and we must not be discouraged if no very great achievements are reserved for our generation. "Show thy servants thy work, and their children thy glory," may be the most appropriate prayer for us. And if certain aspects of the immediate future appear somewhat dark, we must remember in the first place that perhaps the worst moments of life are those in which we are weeping over misfortunes which never come, and secondly that to God, who has all eternity to work in, it matters little if His purposes are thwarted for a season; nor need it trouble us very much if we believe in our own immortality.

II

THE SPIRIT OF THE AGES

SINCE I gave my first lecture, which I imagined to be a quiet little talk to a few London ladies, several of them my friends, I seem to have emerged into a publicity which I neither expected nor desired. I have found myself dubbed "the gloomy dean," in contrast with certain more popular ecclesiastics, who, because they can always conscientiously shout with the largest crowd, are naturally cheerful deans.

Well, you who heard me last week know that I was only telling you (1) not to use catchwords till you are quite sure what you mean by them; (2) not to worship "the idols of the marketplace" till you are quite sure what they are made of.

The title which you chose for me put me on the defensive. I am in the middle of proving to you that the Spirit of the Ages is a much better Spirit to co-operate with than the Spirits of this particular Age.

But since, among scores of more or less interesting letters, which I have not time to answer, there have been a few containing mere abuse, as if it were a kind of impiety not to float with the stream, a feat which any dead dog can accomplish, and a kind of treason not to lick the dirty boots of our masters for the time being, a complaisance which every live dog is eager to perform, I will ask you to recall a certain historical episode.

Once upon a time there was a great Prophet and Teacher, who lived in an age when His countrymen were very much excited by the hope of a wonderful social and political deliverance, which they wrongly believed to be close at hand. He told them that their millennium was not coming at all, nor anything like it; but He added that He had been commissioned to bring them something better, namely, a spiritual and moral emancipation which would make life happy and blessed for them, whatever earthly troubles they might have to endure. This "unpatriotic pessimism" was too much for His countrymen; so, although they approved of the excellent moral tone of His sermons, they had Him crucified. But before He died, He founded an order of teachers, who were to go on delivering His message, and no other, while the world should last. He was determined that no one should undertake this business without knowing exactly what he was in for. "If," He said, "they have called the Master of the house Beelzebub (that is, a devil), how much more them of his household?" "Ye shall be hated of all men for my name's sake." "Woe unto you when all men shall speak well of you, for so did their fathers unto the false prophets." Now it happens that your present lecturer pledged himself, nearly twenty-five years ago, to preach this message to the best of his ability. I admit that I am glad that crucifixion has gone out of fashion; but I hereby tell my critics that I do not care two straws for any abuse and unpopularity that I may incur in preaching the Gospel of the Kingdom as I believe our Master intended it to be preached. That Gospel I believe to be pretty well comprehended in sayings like these: "The Kingdom of heaven is within you." "My Kingdom is not of this world." "Is not the life more than meat, and the body than raiment?" "The Kingdom of God is not eating and drinking, but righteousness and peace and joy in the Holy Ghost." Holding these views and this commission, if I see large numbers of people being fed up with hopes which can only end in bitter disappointment, I shall take leave to show them "a more excellent way," not in season and out of season, but certainly when I am specially invited to talk about the co-operation of the Church with the Spirit of the Age.

. . . . . .

It is decidedly easier to know human nature in general than a man or woman in particular. And in the same way it is, I think, easier to discern the general purposes and methods of the Spirit of the Ages, or, in more Christian language, the will of God for humanity at large, than to detach truth from falsehood, good from evil, in the weltering chaos of conflicting opinions and opposing tendencies which surges round us in the particular generation in which we live. Leibnitz's saying about Nature—that she is simple as regards principles, and endlessly varied as regards their application—is equally true of the spiritual development of humanity. It is not very difficult to trace, in broad outline, the portrait of the "perfect man"—the human being who realises the idea of what a man should be. But it is very hard indeed to lay down detailed rules of conduct for the ideal Englishman at the beginning of the Twentieth Century.

"The spiritual life is a development of the organised universe [says Eucken: *The New Idealism*, p. 10], a development which takes place in man, communicates itself to man, but is never merely man's production. The spiritual life would be wholly incomprehensible, nor could it ever become a power in us, were it not independent of us in our merely human capacity, if the collective life which it reveals were not native to reality itself, and possessed of its own intrinsic principles of connexion." The spiritual life is the highest form of natural life, though, as Eucken is never tired of insisting, it is a new kind of life, a veritable new birth which makes us new men. In becoming a spiritual being, mankind reached full growth, he entered upon his adult career, and his inheritance.

We can no longer look upon our race as the one important part of God's creation, nor upon our earth as the centre of the universe. There are probably countless other races of intelligent and moral creatures, some more and others less highly developed than ourselves, living upon the planets which we may assume to be whirling round the myriads of stars which we can see, and the millions of stars which we do not see. Not that sentient life is more than a brief episode in the career of any planet. During the vast majority of the ages during which it rolls through space it is dead, or rather asleep, frozen into darkness and stillness until some chance collision inaugurates a new era by turning the two colliding bodies into incandescent gas. God, having all eternity at His disposal, is infinitely prodigal of time. Whether the whole process ever had a beginning or will have an end, we know not. Most philosophical and scientific thinkers seem to believe that it had no beginning and will have no end, in spite of the gloomy prognostications founded on the second law of thermo-dynamics.

Is there any intelligent purpose in this strange dance of worlds, or is it only in the human soul that the intelligence and moral character of God are reflected? In what sense can we say with Tennyson that "Through the ages one unceasing purpose runs"?

If the cosmic process is endless, I do not see how *one* unceasing purpose can run through it. For a purpose, it seems to me, is necessarily and essentially finite. It proceeds from one point to another point, from inception to fulfilment. Either, then, the cosmic process has a beginning and an end in time, or the will of God is expressed not in one single all-embracing purpose, but in a plurality of finite purposes, which of course may overlap and interlace, small schemes forming part of great ones. This latter view is what I hold myself. I believe that God has many purposes in His creation, some of which are, so far as we can tell, independent of each other, while others are intertwined. Every one of these purposes has its fulfilment in the time-series, after which it takes its place in the eternal order. Its life in time is over.

I venture to think that of all ways of trying to understand the world-order, the most satisfactory and the most fruitful is that which thus conceives of it as "a system of ends rather than of causes," to use an expression of Lord Haldane's, as a vast kingdom of finite purposes, the realisation of which is the sole reason why the time-series exists. Whether each purpose is unique, or whether the same idea is repeated during the life of the universe, is a question which we cannot answer, and which does not matter to us much.

We Christians all believe that God has a purpose in creating each individual; that He has before Him a definite type of character which He wishes you and me and every one to exhibit —not the same type for all, but a special type for each. We believe that we were sent into the world to work out our salvation by conforming our life and conduct to this type. In the words of a Stoic poet, we each have to discover

"quem te Deus esse iussit, et humana qua parte locatus es in re."

When our short lives are over we take our places in the eternal order, and our rank or fate in the world of spirits is determined by the degree in which we have fulfilled or frustrated the design of our Creator, the extent to which we have finished or neglected the work that He gave us to do. Well, I believe that we are justified in inferring, from this analogy of the individual life, that something of the same kind is true of God's dealings with the human race as a whole. I believe that God has a purpose, an idea, of the life of humanity as a whole—a scheme of discipline and of gradual progress towards relative perfection which He has designed to be worked out in human history. The analogy of the individual life forbids us to suppose that the Divine scheme is necessarily to be realised in its entirety. As individuals may grieve and quench and even blaspheme against the Spirit, so humanity might fall short of the grace of God and disappoint its Creator. But it seems to me a matter of reasonable faith to believe that the *great* design will as a whole be realised. I cannot now discuss the formidable problem—the problem of evil—which the admission of the possibility of even partial failure raises. That problem indeed seems to be insoluble. Suffice it to say that both experience and revelation teach us that men are free to choose, and free to choose wrong.

But this view of humanity as in a sense an unit—of the whole life of the human race as the working out of a definite finite purpose or idea of the Creator, has several important consequences.

First, it involves the admission of a real progress in the human race, which gives a meaning to history. The fact of progress has not been universally admitted, and is denied by some of our most recent thinkers, such as Driesch, whose *Gifford Lectures,* in spite of their difficult style, are well worthy of attention. He apparently agrees with Goethe, who declared that "mankind is always advancing, but man always remains the same." That is to say, on this theory, progress is only by accumulation, not by inner transformation. We seem to be better and wiser than the men of a thousand years ago, because we can stand on the shoulders of past generations. As regards the acquisition of useful knowledge and experience, we can begin where our fathers left off. Their discoveries do not die with them; their mistakes are on record for us to profit by. This, we are told, is sufficient to account for the appearance of progress. But there has been, on this theory, no evolution of man himself; "man always remains the same." I confess that I am predisposed to reject this view because it contradicts the belief in a divine purpose for humanity which I greatly cherish; because it deprives history of all interest and the time-process of all rational meaning; because it quenches the hope of any real improvement in human character, and leaves our well-being dependent on mere accumulations of knowledge which may be lost in the future, as similar accumulations have been lost in the past; because it encourages us to pin our hopes for social amelioration solely on improved environment—on nurture and not on nature; because, finally, it ignores the work of the Holy Spirit upon the soul—a work which I at least regard as a continuation of the redemptive process inaugurated by the incarnation of Christ, an initiation of humanity into the higher spiritual life, for which the whole previous history of the race was a preparation and education. But apart from any predisposition against it, surely history shows that this view is too pessimistic. Civilised men are on an average morally better than savages. Social life has a moralising influence; and members of a civilised society undergo a real adaptation to fit themselves for it. (The latest biology, let me say parenthetically, allows a far larger function to adaptation than the strict Darwinians were willing to admit.) And though we rightly feel the onesidedness of such uncritical books as Brace's *Gesta Christi*, in which every victory of morality and good sense is put down to Christianity, it is surely within the truth to say that the leaven which Christ hid nineteen hundred years ago in three measures of meal has made some progress towards leavening the lump.

But though the progress of human nature itself, apart from its accumulations, is, if our theory is correct, a fact, we must discount very seriously some of the hopes that have been built upon the supposed law of progress. In the first place, there is a limit to it. There is a limit of time, because, as I have argued, every purpose must be finite, and every finite purpose has a temporal term. We know, too, that a time will come when this planet will no longer be tenantable by human beings. This drives us to the "sure and certain hope" of eternal life; otherwise the whole process would be irrational. Why should we labour and deny ourselves, if the only result of our trouble will be to increase the expensiveness of the final crash? Humanity is intended to do and be something which God values, on this earth and in time; after which our race will pass away, and our place will know us no more. Here we have no continuing city; but when our earthly tabernacle is dissolved, we have a house not made with hands, eternal in the heavens. There is the same law for the race in general as for the individual in particular.

Secondly, progress is neither necessary nor uniform. It is quite possible, though it would be a blow to my faith to have to believe it, that humanity may come to a stand, and live for the future in a fixed stationary condition, like the polities of bees and ants, which have a real civilisation, but apparently an absolutely unprogressive one. Variations, if they ever occur, must, in insect civilisation, be promptly eliminated. But in any case, there have been in the past real "dark ages" of regression. It is certainly not true that each generation shows an advance upon its predecessor. For instance, the state of morals described by Gregory of Tours, even after the triumph of the Catholic Church, is quite appalling—much worse than the condition of Pagan antiquity. The history of religion, I regret to say, is seldom one of advance. We find sporadic efforts of genius, which for a time raise the tone of religious life and thought; and then a rapid declension to a lower type. In Jewish history we see how the Church of the prophets sank into the Church of the chief priests and lawyers. The purity of the Apostolic Age was too soon lost. So were the reforms of St. Francis. Sir W. M. Ramsay, who is no prophet of pessimism, says in his book *The Cities of St. Paul,* "The history of religion among men is, with the rarest exceptions, a history of degeneration." I venture to think this too strong, though there is too much justification for it. For, somehow or other, the general movement of the race is upward, not downward. Inspired prophets make good again the losses of institutional religion.

Thirdly, what we now know of the history of humanity prepares us to find improvement excessively slow. I do not know how long human beings, who would pass as human, are supposed to have existed. I suppose 150,000 years is not very far from the mark. Civilisation has been entirely the work of the last 10,000 years, a sudden burst of apparent progress after a long period of apparent stagnation. The larger part, though not the whole, of this apparent progress must surely be merely cumulative—pseudo-evolution. I am afraid existing conditions do not favour any acceleration of real improvement; but I hope that in the future, when both ends and means are seen more clearly, there *may* be a quickening of the pace. No one, I suppose, could predict how long the race has yet to live. The discovery of radio-activity has upset the old calculations. But it would not be rash to say that civilisation, which began in certain river-valleys about 10,000 years ago, is probably still only in its childhood. And the Church, so far from saying in the words of a foolish hymn,—

"Far down the ages now, my journey well nigh done,"

has only begun to crawl and babble. Her life lies before her, not behind her. The "traditions of the first six centuries" are the traditions of the rattle and feeding-bottle.

Another very interesting reflexion is that the breathless hurry with which mankind has been advancing during the historical period has left his physical and psychical constitution far behind. Nature cannot change in such a hurry. Many of you have probably read Metchnikoff's curious and interesting book called *The Nature of Man*, in which he points out how many maladaptations there are in our physical constitution, in relation to the duties which we now lay upon our bodies. An appendix is as superfluous at the end of the human cæcum as at the end of a volume of light literature. We do not in the least require 26 feet of tubing to help us to digest our food, though the whole apparatus of pipes may have been useful when we ate grass. There are several other examples of the same thing. It is as if, when we wanted a motor car, we had to put up with a superannuated traction-engine. A great deal of what we theologians call " sin " is due to the same causes. Certain appetites which in the savage state are only just strong enough to preserve the tribe from diminution, are inconveniently insistent in civilisation. The competitive and acquisitive instinct which made its possessor very useful to his tribe thousands of years ago, is a public nuisance when it inspires the career of a Jay Gould or Rockefeller. Reverence for tradition, and implicit belief in the wisdom of antiquity, which kept the young and tender plant of inherited culture from being trampled out of existence, is now a doubtful advantage when it determines the counsels of an episcopal conclave, or a Representative Church Council. We must try to look upon these evils with an understanding eye, and with infinite patience.

The Spirit of the Ages is not going to hurry herself because we have only seventy years or so in which to watch her operations.

Again, our view that reality is essentially a system of ends or purposes—that the course of nature is radically teleological—obliges us to take a view of evolution which differs considerably from that of the straitest sect of the Darwinians, but which agrees very well with more recent theories, now dominant at least in Germany. We have probably been led by the Darwinians to attribute too much importance to natural selection (this I said, I remember, in my first address). Natural selection no doubt eliminates inferior variations; but we have now a right to believe—the evidence for such a belief seems to be accumulating every year—that each species has (unconsciously, of course) a tendency—we might almost say a desire—to realise a certain type. Living beings strive to live, not anyhow, but in a certain manner. I will hazard no theory about parasites and other species which seem to have degenerated: we cannot tell whether their Maker regards them as "fallen," or whether He intended them to live ignobly at the expense of their hosts. But man has never been content merely to exist: he has always wished to live a human life. The Spirit of the Ages has set a goal before him, a model for him to copy, a standard for him to reach. The struggle for life has in his case been a struggle for a rational life, and ultimately for a spiritual life.

Lastly, I ask you to consider how our belief that reality is a system of ends, a concatenation of finite purposes willed by the Creator and appointed by Him to be actualised in time, must necessarily affect our judgment of all particular events. We may conveniently draw a distinction between phenomena and facts. A *phenomenon* is a particular occurrence, viewed in isolation, as if it were not part of a system. A *fact* is the working out of some unitary idea. If our view is correct, phenomena are only abstractions: we do not get at the truth of things by regarding them in isolation, or in any other way except as links in a chain by which some particular thought in the mind of God, some particular design in the will of God, is being expressed and actualised. A *fact* has always a beginning, middle, and end, and until we know the end as well as the beginning, we are not in a position to estimate the fact correctly. Now all facts that are really interesting are still unfinished. The world is still in the making, and mankind is in the making too. If it is the characteristic of a teleological series that its rationality is not intelligible until the last term is available for observation, it is no wonder that many things in our experience perplex and baffle us. It is also just what we should expect, that the largest and most far-reaching and exalted of God's purposes, those which have in view the representation and realisation of the grandest ideas and the most divine designs, are precisely those which cause us most difficulty. "What I do thou knowest not now, but thou shalt know hereafter." Even the past is not over and done with when it forms part of a living, growing organic scheme. This is the philosophical proof of the doctrine of repentance and forgiveness. In an organic whole losses may be repaired, waste products utilised. God may even "restore to us the years that the locust hath eaten." I need not point out how much encouragement may be derived from this doctrine by those who are troubled by existing tendencies, which seem to them to portend nothing but disaster.

> "The time is out of joint :—O cursed spite,
> That ever I was born to set it right."

Happily, we were not born to do anything of the kind. We are too apt to think that the sun will be extinguished when our farthing rushlight goes out. In the days of the Commonwealth, Bulstrode Whitelocke, ambassador to the Hague, was tossing about through the night in anxiety about the condition of his country and Church. An old servant, lying in the same room, addressed him: "Sir, may I ask you a question?" "Certainly," replied the ambassador. "Sir, did God govern the world well before you came into it?" "Undoubtedly." "And will He rule the world well when you have gone out of it?" "Undoubtedly." "Then, Sir, can you not trust Him to rule the world well while you are in it?" The tired ambassador turned on his side and fell asleep. The Spirits of the Age may be phenomena, not facts; the Spirit of the Ages has before now turned the fierceness of man to God's praise; and after subduing the ape and tiger she may, as Bishop Creighton said, have the same success with that more intractable animal, the donkey.

The historical period, brief as it has been in comparison with the tremendous vistas of time which physics and geology lay open before us, has witnessed one real addition to human faculties which is of the highest importance. The religious sense, the spiritual life, is nothing less than a glimpse into a new and better world, a foretaste of higher gifts and higher possibilities. Faith, in the beautiful words of Jacobi, is "the reflexion of the Divine knowledge and will in the finite spirit of man." The appearance of this faculty, and its development, are alone a sufficient proof that progress is not merely a possibility, but a fact. In the spiritual life, the purpose of God for the human race, which for long ages had been working unconsciously in the half-formed intellects of our humble progenitors, has become partly self-conscious. God has at last allowed us to see part of His plan for us. He has lifted one corner of the curtain which hides the eternal world from the creatures of time. The promise of the Johannine Christ is fulfilled: "Henceforth I call you not servants," &c. The dawning of the God-consciousness was, I suppose, coincident with the appearance of *reason* as a more serviceable instrument for future progress than *instinct*. Instinct may, as Bergson argues, be a more efficient tool in some ways; but reason has the decisive advantage of being self-directing: it is infinitely more adaptable than instinct. The consciousness of God, the worship and service of Him, are the highest exercise of reason. This is the child which the Spirit of the Ages has so long been labouring to bring to the birth. It gives us the power of offering to God "reasonable service."

In broad outline, as I said at the beginning of my address, we can see clearly, and express in words, the nature of the revelation which God has given us of Himself. Moral goodness, truth, and beauty have been often said to be the three attributes under which God is known to us; and I do not think that we can improve upon this classification. The three attributes are so far independent that none of them can be regarded as ancillary to another. Each stands and reigns in his own right. But they are so far interdependent that we cannot neglect one without causing the others to suffer. It is quite plain that the "perfect man" must be one whose moral, intellectual, and æsthetic faculties are all fully developed. This gives us, I think, a sufficiently definite standard. Whatsoever things are just and good, whatsoever things are true, whatsoever things are lovely, sublime, and of good report, these things have an absolute value ; these things we are to think of and ponder over ; in the promotion of these within us and without lies the true course of human development.

But we must not forget that the spiritual sense, the God-consciousness, or whatever we like to call it, is a *new* endowment, as compared with our eyes and ears and other senses. We should expect, should we not, to find it feeble and fitful, almost absent in a great many individuals, and strong only in a very few persons who have, as it were, anticipated the course of human evolution? We should expect to find religion clinging for support to other and more firmly established parts of our nature, twining itself round any support which will give it hospitality, entangling itself inextricably with other interests which have but little to do with it, nay, often clinging to a dead stump. Very slowly can it hope to establish itself in human nature, casting its roots downward and bearing fruit upward. This is what we should expect to find, and this is what we actually find. The history of religion is profoundly perplexing and depressing if we look at it in any other way. Looked at in this way, it is not depressing. It only reminds us of a year-old child trying to walk with the help of chairs and tables, and frequently falling " between two stools."

Christianity is not incompatible with belief in evolution, as has been often supposed. We must suppose that the great revelation was made " in the fulness of time," that is to say, at the earliest possible moment. There is no difficulty, even without having recourse to the miraculous, in believing that the greatest and best among the sons of men lived 2000 years ago. We have seen that by far the greater part of apparent progress is mere accumulation, false evolution ; we have seen that the real changes in so short a period as 2000 years must be very slight ; we have also seen that progress is by no means uniform. The greatest sculptors lived much more than 2000 years ago. However, I should of course wish to place the Founder of Christianity in a far more unique position. As St. Augustine says, " He summed up in Himself the long series of human life." In Him the Spirit of the Ages—the Logos, as St. John calls it—tabernacled among us.

My main object in this address has been to urge you to take *long* views: to look before and after, as far down the vista of the ages as you can in both directions. I do not know why it is that we attribute such an exaggerated importance to the age in which we happen to be living. When we are in a railway train, the fields which we are passing seem to be real, while the sea which we crossed a few hours ago has become a portion and parcel of the dreadful past: but we know that that is only illusion. The sea is there all the time. And so, in God's sight, the past and future are there all the time; 1911 is just as important or unimportant a year as 1811 or 2011. If we seriously believe in our own immortality, we can feel this and take comfort in it—if not, we cannot. But if we are immortal spirits, we should not degrade ourselves by worrying too much about the Zeitgeist. Do not sacrifice your own soul to the fads of this generation. They are not worth it. Your own spirit—the microcosm; the spirit of the ages—the macrocosm; these are eternal verities. Passing events are only important in so far as they are *not* "passing," but linked on to some great idea which is working itself out—some idea the beginning of which we did not hear, the end of which we shall not see, and the meaning of which we very imperfectly understand.

III

THE CHURCH

THIS has been by far the most difficult to write of my four addresses. I would gladly have shirked speaking about the Church, and confined myself to the practical question, "What can we do?" But it is really waste of time to discuss a theme like this without defining our terms. We have submitted "the Spirit of the Age" to a searching examination, and have, I hope, at least proved that if there is a single Spirit of the Age she is the spirit of other ages too; and that the Spirit of the Ages is not an easy Spirit to find or to interrogate, since her voice is still and small; she does not strive nor cry, nor cause her voice to be heard in the street. Now, if we are to do any good at all by this discussion, if we are to clear our minds of cant and confusion, if we are to face facts as they are, which is the indispensable preliminary to inducing them to change into what we would have them to be, we must apply an equally searching investigation to the word "Church," the other party to the pleasant scheme of "co-operation" which is up with alien alloy. The teaching of Christ Himself was spiritual religion of the purest water. But even He took no trouble, it appears, to separate it from the pathetic Messianic expectation of the unhappy Jewish people, from whom the Romans were soon about to "take away their place and nation." His earliest disciples, in the years following His departure from the earth, seem to have lived as orthodox Jewish mystics, conforming to ceremonies which meant little to them, and living on the hope of a speedy deliverance. The Church began as a mere stop-gap till the Kingdom of God should come; but it was so sanctified by the love and holiness which radiated from the memories of Christ, and the echoes of His voice, that a beautiful brotherhood grew up in His name, which lived more and more on the presence of the Spirit, which was a growing reality, and less and less on the fading Apocalyptic dream. So the society consolidated, with its necessary officers and discipline; and so through the activities of St. Paul it became an European religion, an aspirant to be the dominant faith of the Græco-Roman world.

This transplantation from Asia to Europe has been the greatest change that Christianity has ever undergone. Our religion died in the country of its origin; in the adjoining Asiatic countries it fell after an ignominiously feeble resistance before the onslaught of a genuinely

Semitic religion—that of Islam. It is now the least Semitic, the least Asiatic, of all creeds, so that there is no part of the world where the prospects of Christian missions seem so unhopeful as that in which the light of the Gospel first shone. This does not at all imply that there is a cleft between the Church and Christ, as Professor Burkitt and others have said. Christ Himself was no Semite in character or teaching; writers like Houston Chamberlain, regardless of Church tradition, have argued that, as a Galilean, he probably had not a drop of Jewish blood in his veins. The Gospel really only came to its own, was only understood, when it was finally disconnected from Jewish nationalism.

Christianity then became the religion of the Greeks and Latins—not of course of the Hellenes and Romans, for those two nations were practically extinct. And as the Empire fell apart into two sections, the Greek provinces with their capital on the Bosporus, the Latin provinces with their capital on the Tiber, so the Church too was disrupted in exactly the same manner. It followed the dividing lines not of doctrine but of language. In what sense then (we are asked) can we maintain that the Latin Church, or the Greek Church, is the heir and representative of Christ's little flock of Oriental peasants?

It has sometimes been said that the Church fought and conquered Isis and Mithra with their own weapons: that Christianity offered all the same attractions as the other syncretistic creeds of the later Empire, and outbid them. But this is not, I think, the truth—at any rate not the whole truth. From the first the Christians felt themselves a people *apart* in the Roman Empire. They could make no terms with the other religions; they could not tolerate them as rivals. The Romans nicknamed the Christians "The Third Race" (*tertia gens*), the "second" being the Jews. With all the adaptations which made Christianity attractive to the European subjects of the Empire, and unpalatable to the Asiatic, there was a consciousness, a conviction, that Christianity was the custodian of an unique divine tradition, with sanctions and a moral standard of its own. The Pagans understood this instinctively; they felt the menace, and so they were driven to persecute, spasmodically and ineffectually; for religious persecution was contrary to all their traditions, and they could not carry such a policy through. At last came the inevitable concordat when Diocletian's persecution had failed, and then followed an era of wholesale forced conversions which nearly half-paganised the Church. The Pagan, however, as a rule, did not care to die for his faith, just because he had no intention of giving it up. The *nomina* were changed; the *numina* remained the same, or nearly so.

Above all, the Pagan subject of the Empire was not required to abandon his faith in the one deity who, unlike the denizens of the old Italian pantheon whose names figured in the *indigitamenta*, was by no means a colourless abstraction. Very little Roman blood, perhaps, flowed in the veins of the fifth century Spaniard or Gaul, or even Italian. Slavery had flooded Western Europe with Orientals, invasion with Germans. But pride in Rome was a religion among its subjects everywhere. Claudian's magnificent boast—

> " Haec est in gremium victos quae sola recepit
> humanumque genus communi nomine fovit
> matris non dominae ritu, civesque vocavit
> quos domuit, nexuque pio longinqua revinxit,"

did not go beyond the truth. Awe and reverence, pride, even love, had gathered round the Eternal City, the unique magnificence and overwhelming achievements of which seemed even more tremendous than they were to those who only knew a quarter of the earth's surface. The barbarians were as much awestruck by Rome as her own subjects. And when the sceptre at last fell from her nerveless hands, what more natural than to do homage to the priestly Cæsar who sat in the Eternal City? The Roman Church is not merely, as Hobbes said, the ghost of the dead Empire sitting crowned and sceptred amid the ruins thereof; it is the Empire itself come to life again. Its whole policy, aims, and methods are those of the Roman *imperium*. Obedience rather than conviction is required; dissent is punished as treason; a state of permanent warfare exists against all outside the pale, for they too are rebels against an empire which is *de jure* co-extensive with the world. The property of an enemy is *res nullius*. The prætorian guard, the legions, the proconsuls, the imperial court, all have their parallels. It is magnificent; but what has it all to do with the Sermon on the Mount?

Meanwhile, in the Eastern half of the Empire the Church, where it was not overwhelmed by Mohammed and his fanatical soldiery, sank into a truly Chinese immobility, in contented alliance with the secular arm. Byzantine Christianity, as it existed in the East Roman Empire till 1453, may still be studied, almost unchanged, in Russia. It is difficult for Western Europeans to form a just estimate of this Church. Travellers say that devotion is widespread and fervent, and that religion is a real comfort and support to the Russian peasant under the hardships which he endures; but Christianity seems to have sunk permanently, in the East, into a mystery-cult which scarcely attempts to influence conduct, like the popular religions of the East in antiquity. To the superficial observer, at any rate, it is far more like the old Pagan religion in a Christian dress than anything else. The average Greek will rob you whenever he gets the chance, and he will knife a fellow-countryman on very slight provocation; but nothing will induce him to eat a sandwich in Lent. Again, what has this kind of religion to do with Jesus Christ?

Nevertheless, the gift of Pentecost has never been withdrawn in either Church. Not in the policy of diplomatists, not in the decisions of councils, not in wars of religion and forcible suppressions of heresy, must His guidance and sanctifying power be looked for, but in the unbroken succession of saints who have been the true runners in the torch race, the bearers of the light which, once kindled, shall never be put out. These saints, unless they have confined themselves to devotion and contemplation or to works of charity, have been as often persecuted as sheltered by the official Church; but the Church may claim the credit of having taught them, and of having generally retained their allegiance. No Church that can produce saints is spiritually dead or morally bankrupt.

The strength of Christianity has been largely due to the blend of the original Semitic element, which, we must remember, included and includes the sacred books of the Jews, with the Græco-Roman traditions, intellectually and æsthetically so splendid, into which the new religion entered.

It is true that Judaism was not the old faith of the free Hebrew nation, and that Hellenistic paganism was not the faith of the free Greeks. Still less was Romanism the creed of the free Romans. I think it is permissible for a Christian to admit what is difficult for a historian to deny—that none of these three nations were allowed to bring their best to build up the grand edifice called the Catholic Church. All three had passed through disillusionment and defeat; all three were, in a sense, in a state of senile decay. The Greek race had proved the truth of Homer's words, that the gods take away half of a man's manhood when he loses his freedom. Their literature and art had become feeble and imitative; their philosophy had said its last word of permanent value when Plotinus died in 270. But in truth the race was almost extinct; the Hellenists were not Hellenes. The churchmen of Judaism, whom John the Baptist tried in vain to arouse and alarm, had long forgotten the voice of the prophets; theirs was a religion of priests, scholastic theologians, and Biblical commentators. That was a large part of their legacy to Christianity. Even St. Paul did not succeed in banishing the Law from the Gospel. As for Rome, just as Greece expired in giving birth to Hellenism, so the Eternal City was the mausoleum rather than the citadel of the sturdy race of soldier-farmers whose name was a terror from one end of the Mediterranean to another. The great machine remained—her law and discipline and traditions of government—but the men were gone.

So, amid the last sighs of the three great creative nations of antiquity, the Catholic Church spread its wings over an exhausted and nerveless world. It bears all the marks of its early surroundings. Græco-Roman Catholicism is not a religion which could ever have been evolved by free men. Obedience, loyalty, patient endurance, self-devotion, gentle piety, all the virtues of the servile condition—these it could preach and practise. But "self-reverence, self-knowledge, self-control," truthfulness and honour, fair play and fidelity to obligations, a social conscience and indignation at public crimes—above all, that intellectual honesty which dreads what Plato calls "the lie in the soul," even more than the lie on the lips—these never have been and are not the virtues which that type of Christianity tends to foster. The typical Catholic has many fine qualities, but, as Newman saw clearly, he is something radically different, down to the roots of his character, from what the Northern European means by a free man and a good citizen.

How strange a thing it is that this Church, the product of racial experiences so ancient, so rich, and so tragic, should have been, in God's providence, the schoolmaster of the "young barbarians" of Northern Europe! With the conversion of the Teutonic races a wholly new and most disturbing, disintegrating element intruded itself into Christendom. So far, Christianity had had to deal with mature or even senescent civilisations, but now a new type began to press its claim—a people in all the freshness of its early youth, whose spiritual individuality was becoming ever more definitely marked; a people, moreover, presenting many marks of superiority, greater depth and tenderness of feeling, more truth and inwardness in the soul's relations to God, a stronger desire for a freer individual development, a boundless seriousness of personal conviction;[1] a people, moreover, whose ancestors had never trembled at the lictor's rods or fled before the tramp of the legions; a people who had never been in bondage to any man, and whose first thought on seeing Rome was probably that of Blücher surveying London from the top of St. Paul's: "Heavens! what a place to sack!" No wonder that the priestly Cæsar at Rome had to lament a greater disaster than the victory of Arminius over the troops of Augustus, "Quintilius Varus, give me back my legions!"

What has Northern Europe, emancipated from the yoke and free to follow Christ in

[1] Eucken, *Christianity and the New Idealism*, p. 97.

its own way, made of its opportunities? What are the characteristics of Teutonic Christianity? Strange to say, after all these centuries, it is still too early to answer this question. Ever since the Reformation the Reformed Churches have been in a state of fumbling uncertainty—full of earnestness and deep conviction, but quite undecided what kind of Church they want, how it ought to be governed, what the conditions of membership should be, and where the seat of authority resides. It is a ludicrous spectacle, if you will—certainly a pathetic one. The well-organised Latins, who have no troubles of this kind, are justified, from their own point of view, in pointing the finger of scorn at us. They have all the advantages of disciplined troops fighting against a mob. It is a situation with which the statesmen of the Empire were quite familiar. Again and again the fair-haired, long-limbed barbarians succumbed to the discipline and tactics of their opponents, and left their bodies to fertilise the fields of Italy.

But let us look at the present situation—as in these addresses I have been asking you to survey every question—as a problem not for one generation or one century only, but as a phase in a long process which had its beginning in the remote past, and will have its end in the remote future. We Northern Europeans are still a young people, comparatively new to civilisation. We were painting ourselves blue and sacrificing our prisoners of war long after the great masterpieces of Greek and Roman literature, which form the staple of our higher education, were composed. We have never quite attained to an indigenous civilisation with independent traditions. We are on the whole ahead of the Latin races, and have left the Eastern Europeans far behind; but we have to go to a remote and alien past for our traditions, especially for our religious traditions. There is no such hide-bound Tory in the world as the religious spirit. It is profoundly uncomfortable if it cannot find or invent a tradition of the elders to justify every article in its creed and every detail in its worship.

So the Reformed Churches have been in trouble from the first. They have not dared to dispense with traditions which are irreconcilable with their own independence; or, if they have, they have drifted hither and thither, and lost their way.

But surely, to the observer with a seeing eye, the appearance presented by the Reformed Churches is not that of an organism which has been broken up and is in process of dissolution, but rather of a number of vigorous and living elements which have not yet succeeded in coalescing. If we believe in liberty, as I for one do heartily, though not in democracy, we cannot doubt that all the intense earnestness, seriousness, and deep sincerity which characterise the religion of Northern Europe will end in bringing order out of chaos. I am quite unable to predict what form that order will take. It will certainly be a new type of Christianity, neither Latin nor Greek, but corresponding to the national character of the English, German, and Dutch peoples. It will, we may presume, be strongly ethical, and marked with that blend of strenuous practicality and high idealism which belongs to our national character. It will be individualistic on its inner side, and actively social on its outer side. Its organisation will be loose, for we English do not love being drilled, and its capacity for collective action limited. Beyond this, I can see no clear indications of the direction in which we are moving.

You will see that I look to the future rather than to the past or present when I try to picture the reality of the Christian Church—the Church as God sees it. Surely no one can suppose that the existing state of Christendom—the fossilised Church of the East, the Cæsarised Church of the Latin West, the chaotic and fissiparous Churches of Northern Europe and America—are anything better than a caricature of what the Church of Christ ought to be and may be. And surely no one with any glimmering of the historical sense can suppose that any offered for our approval and admiration. When we say that "the Church" should co-operate with the Spirit of the Age, what exactly do we mean by the Church?

There are as many different definitions of "the Church" as there are sects in Christendom. Our Nineteenth Article says that "the visible Church of Christ is a congregation of faithful men in the which the pure word of God is preached, and the Sacraments be duly ministered according to Christ's ordinance in all those things that are requisite to the same," a definition which unchurches the Quakers, who have no sacraments, while it judiciously refrains from saying what theological views contradict "the pure word of God," or what institutional and ritual irregularities are fatal to the "due" ministration of the Sacraments. The Bidding Prayer (in the form used in the University Church at Oxford, and sanctioned by the Canons) defines the Holy Catholic Church as "the whole congregation of Christian people dispersed throughout the whole world," a comprehensive and charitable definition which will commend itself at least to theological Liberals. The Roman Church excludes from the Catholic Church all who do not acknowledge the supremacy of the Pope; the Eastern Church, I suppose, puts outside the pale all who hold to the double procession of the Holy Spirit. Some Protestants believe that the Church is invisible, and that God only knows who belong to it. The Plymouth Brethren, I believe, hold that their own sect is " the Church." Lastly, we have all heard of the Scotch lady who believed that the elect consisted of herself and possibly her minister, though she " whiles had doots " about him.

To the observer from outside, Christendom would seem to be split into three main bodies or groups of approximately equal size. These are, of course, the Roman Catholic Church, the Eastern Orthodox Church, and the Protestant Churches, disunited, but conscious of bonds of sympathy and kinship with each other, as contrasted with the self-styled Catholic and Orthodox Churches. Of these three, the Roman Church is still somewhat the largest, and the Eastern Church the smallest, though the enormous birth-rate in Russia may reverse the position within fifty years. Our own Church is a characteristically insular institution, which evades all classification. In its present shape it was the product of a political compromise, which was so framed as to include Catholics who would renounce the Pope, and Puritans who were not anarchists on principle. It is officially Protestant, and dislikes the name. It has framed tests of Catholicity which separate it from the non-Episcopalian Churches, and which are scornfully rejected by all other Catholics. It has been, in a word, the Church of the honestest and most illogical nation on the face of the globe. What it is now, it is very hard to say. If we take the whole English-speaking population together, instead of only the people of England, into our account, we shall find that the Episcopalians have no great superiority over the Methodists and one or two other sects whom we call dissenters, in point of numbers—an unpleasant fact which we too often forget. In the United States we only come seventh, if I remember right, in the list of denominations arranged numerically.

When we cast our eyes over this "whole body of Christian people dispersed throughout the world," and note their mutual antipathies and real divergences, it is somewhat difficult to attach any meaning to the suggestion that "the Church" should co-operate with the Spirit of the Age, or with any other spirit or body that could be found. If the Spirit of the Age threatens to dissolve into the "Legion" that possessed the great herd of swine, the Spirit of the Church seems to have passed into a vast flock of sheep, some scattered over the mountains, and others jealously penned into rival folds. But as we refused to give up the attempt to find some meaning in "the Spirit of the Age," and perhaps were not wholly unsuccessful in our quest, so we will try to bring together in thought the *disjecta membra* of the body which exists to continue the work which Christ began while on earth.

Since we have strenuously maintained that the present has no meaning or importance except as a link in a design which extends probably far into the past and the future ; and since, if there be any great institution which in the eyes of God represents an unitary ideal and purpose, that institution must surely be the Church, let us turn our gaze over that strange, and on the whole melancholy, chapter in the annals of mankind, called Church History. "The Past," says the Abbé Laberthonnière, "by a quite natural inversion, becomes a torch which goes before us to show us our road, a luminous cloud which guides us through the night of time towards the day of eternity."

The key to the whole mystery is that the teaching of Christ, and the revelation which He came to bring, were so far in advance of the capabilities of those who received it, that Christianity from the very beginning was like a tender climbing plant, seeking to twine itself round any existing support that offered itself. This is, I think, a truer way of putting it than to say, as some have done, that the religious education of mankind has been by means of a series of illusions. But in any case the sad result is that we never get Christianity pure, but always mixed one of these will ever annex, convince, or subjugate the rest. The divisions of Christendom are not accidental, but racial and inevitable. The face of Europe will have to be altered before those boundary lines can be obliterated.

But as regards the English-speaking races, is there any reason why our own beloved Church should not in the future regain the position which once was hers, but which she has now lost, that of being the Church of the English nation—nay, far more, of the English-speaking nations? If the sects—those of them that will survive—are ever to be federated, is there any other possible nucleus than the Church which is still, in this country, the greatest religious body, and which by its wise comprehensiveness occupies a more central position than any other Church in Christendom? I am sure that many of you, in considering the problem laid down for us in the title of these addresses—a problem which has engaged the attention of the members of this Society as the topic chosen for consideration this year—took it for granted that "the Church" means the Anglican Church. Well, it has been one of my objects to suggest to you that these things ought not to be taken for granted—that "the Church" and "the Spirit of the Age" are both expressions which need a great deal of critical examination. But that having been done, there is no reason why we should not consider the prospects and possibilities of our own branch of the Church; for, after all, the object of our inquiry is rather practical than theoretical.

We long to see our Church a faithful steward of the revelation brought to humanity by Christ, a true organ of the indwelling Holy Spirit of God; and we long also to see her take her proper place as the representative and exponent of our national Christianity.

Once more I must beg you to take long views—to remember that a hundred years is as nothing in the life of a church or nation. We shall none of us live to see the torn robe of Christ sewn together again. Reunion in the twentieth century is a dream; and impatience on our part may only put it off longer. I think you must admit the justice of this observation. The idea of reunion with Rome on any terms except complete submission is really childish. To hold such an expectation is to show that a person has wholly misunderstood the position and policy of the Roman Church. The claim to an universal spiritual empire is an essential part of her whole system. The claim to possess an absolute monopoly of divine grace is equally essential. It is quite useless to expect recognition as a reward for close imitation, though it may be the sincerest form of flattery. Do you think that the makers of Sunlight Soap would beam on a rival firm which sold a product indistinguishable from their own, and quite as good for cleansing purposes? This perhaps rather brutal analogy hits the nail on the head so exactly that you must please pardon it. Only Rome goes further, and says, "Any other soap leaves you dirtier than you were before." There is absolutely no chance of Rome surrendering her claim to a monopoly of Catholic rights and privileges, or of accepting any terms short of absolute submission. If any terms short of this were offered by her, it would be with the intention of withdrawing the concessions as soon as they had served their turn. And I need not repeat my reasons for being convinced that the English people are no more likely to pay homage to an Italian priest than taxes to an Italian king —though we all like the Italians, and acknowledge that we owe them a great deal. We do not hear so much now of a *rapprochement* with the Eastern Church, a very pleasing and romantic idea, especially to those who, like myself, very much prefer the Greek Fathers and their theology to the Latin. In this scheme nothing more than mutual recognition is thought of, which makes the idea more reasonable; but I cannot think that we should gain much by associating with the State-Church of a semi-barbarous autocracy, sunk in intellectual torpor and gross superstition. The notion almost reminds us of the cruel jest of

Mezentius, who bound the living bodies of his enemies to corpses. There remains the notion of reunion with the Protestant dissenters, who, we are reminded, are busy federating among themselves. So they are; but it is painfully like the alliance between Russia, Prussia, and Austria preparatory to the partition of Poland. Can we fancy the king of that luckless country breaking into their conclave, and saying, "Gentlemen, I have always looked upon you as my dear brethren. Why should not I come in and make a fourth in your fraternal gatherings?" Well, unfortunately there is this slight objection, that the whole object of the fraternisation is the dismemberment of their dear brother. The time may come—and I hope will come—when the immense majority of English Christians may be content to worship under the same roof; but assuredly we shall not live to see it, and overtures to the other Protestant bodies seem to me, I regret to say, quite premature.

Reunion then, in the sense of fusion with any other Church or Churches, is not a question of practical politics. But let us remember that all good Christians in England are our brethren and have a claim to individual recognition as good Christians. I entirely agree with the words—I forget who uttered them—that the idea of a common Christianity, behind all denominational loyalties, is one which we should steadily hold before ourselves, and encourage by every means in our power.

Let us further remember, with a view to hastening the happy healing of our unhappy divisions—which we pray and hope for, but shall not live to see—how very partial, how very external, almost superficial, those divisions are. Has the Church of Christ ever been divided in the chambers where men shut their door and pray to their Father who is in secret? Do we not all pray the same prayers—at least the same prayer of prayers? Has it ever been divided in the service of praise and thanksgiving? How many of us know or care which hymns in "Ancient and Modern" were written by Roman Catholics, which by Anglicans, and which by Dissenters? Has it ever been divided in the shelves where we keep our books of devotion? *The Imitation of Christ*, Taylor's *Holy Living and Dying*, *The Counsels of Father John Sergieff of Cronstadt*, Penn's *No Cross no Crown* jostle each other near our bedhead, and do not quarrel. The mystics all tell the same tale. They have climbed the same mountain, and their witness agrees together. All ages, denominations, and languages are blended harmoniously on that Jacob's ladder which scales the heavens in far other fashion than is ever dreamed of by the builders of Babel. Has Christendom ever been divided in the world of letters? Do not Biblical scholars, historians, philosophers forget their denominational differences, and work side by side in the cause of truth? Lastly, are we divided in philanthropy and social service? Do we not unite, naturally and spontaneously, in the warfare against vice, crime, and injustice? These are no slight bonds of union. They embrace by far the greater part of our life as children of God and brethren to each other. Is it not much that we already have in common? Let us not magnify the institutional barriers which part us at public worship, but at no other times. If the Church of the future will, we hope, be co-extensive with all who love the Lord Jesus Christ in incorruptness; if this is the goal towards which we are moving, however slowly; if this is the idea of the Church which already exists in the mind of God as a fact; let us press forward thither in heart and mind; let us anticipate that which will surely come to pass, and which, when it has come to pass, will make what is now the present appear in quite a new light; let us keep that "ideal of a Christian Church" ever before us, gazing upon it with that eye of faith which gives substance to things hoped for, and conviction to things not seen.

IV
WHAT CAN WE DO?

I HAVE been dealing rather roughly and disrespectfully with some idols of the market-place, before whom I suspect that some of you are in the habit of throwing flowers or grains of incense. You have not, I hope, inferred that I am flippant or cynical about the possibility of doing good in our generation, and doing it as church-people. It is not so; but the market-place is just now unusually full of idols, some of which badly want breaking. Besides, what is the use of retailing once more those unctuous commonplaces about the downfall of individualism, the duty of trusting the people, the Church's care for the suffering and toiling masses, and the recovery of the idea of corporate unity? Shibboleths and catchwords are useful as labels —(those who utter them we call our friends, those who don't are enemies or suspects)—as missiles, as war-cries (to excite us to a Christian pitch of pugnacity); and sometimes they are very soothing, when like-minded persons get together and administer them to each other; but they have the most fatal effect on sane thinking. If the devil invented partisan labels—and I think he must have done so—it was one of the cleverest tricks he ever played. In practice, I think these shibboleths or platitudes cover much confusion of mind and irrationality of conduct. So I have treated the so-called spirits of the age with considerable freedom. I have declined to burn incense to democracy, or socialism, or "corporate unity," or any of them. The Spirit of the Age, I have maintained, is no true spirit unless she is also the Spirit of the Ages. Her aims are not bounded by this generation, or this century. Her thoughts are much deeper, her outlook much wider. We must probe deep to discover what she thinks and intends.

And "the Church" must not be identified quite unhesitatingly with any particular institution or denomination, nor with tendencies which seem to be dominant in our generation. The Church is an idea in the mind of God, a vast design which is to be worked out in time, requiring probably tens of thousands of years to reach its full development—its "nature," as Aristotle would say. We are not in a position to dogmatise about the Church, because by far the longer portion of its history—that portion, too, which will explain and give its character to the whole—is still in the unknown future. The true Church of the present consists, if we could see it, in those elements in our religious societies, which are capable of being worked up into the Church of the future: the gold, silver, costly marbles, which will survive the testing fire, and will be thought worthy of a place in the temple of God, which is being slowly built upon the one foundation which has been laid once for all. We can judge pretty well what are good materials; it is the designs of our little architects which give us pause. They constantly have to be pulled down, with great trouble and loss of time. And when we see these architects ambitiously building against each other, we rather grudge them the admirable material which they are often able to get, though it is usually mixed with very inflammable stuff—wood, hay, and stubble. Shall we put it thus,—That all which is truly Christian in our age is part of the Church, and belongs to the Church; but it is not yet built up into its final position as a portion of the "glorious Church" (ἔνδοξος ἐκκλησία) which is one day to be, but is not yet?

Remembering, then, that we are much better judges of good and bad material than of the way in which the wise Master-Builder will ultimately decide to use the good material, what can we do to help things forward in our generation? Can the Church of England, in its "corporate" (blessed word!) capacity, do any-

WHAT CAN WE DO? 69

thing to help this country to work out its salvation and finish the work that God gave it to do? Let me first indicate three pitfalls which we shall do well to avoid, and then (at last! you will say) come to a constructive policy.

There are three blunders which a Church is prone to make when it aspires to influence the world as an institution. These three are wonderfully symbolised by the three temptations of our Lord. The narrative of the Temptation, when read in this light, as a warning to the Church of the three insidious traps which the devil intended to set for her, is one of the most remarkable passages in the New Testament. First of all is the temptation to try to reach men's souls through their stomachs, to make a bid for popular favour by offering material advantages. There are very many irreligious people who would be quite ready to say with Jacob, "If the Lord will give me food to eat and raiment to put on, then shall the Lord be my God." This is the false road to success, symbolised by the first temptation. There never was a time when the temptation was so great as it is to-day. The Church as an institution has always been disposed to truckle to the powers that be. I need give no instances of this humiliating and indisputable truth. Formerly it was "the right divine of kings to govern wrong," that resounded from every pulpit. Now that the masses are becoming conscious of the power which democracy puts into their hands, now that they are waking up to the fact that they have their former masters on the hip, the devil whispers insidiously that the Church may make the most of the obviously anti-plutocratic leanings of the Founder, and do a good stroke of business for itself at the same time. Our clergy are positively tumbling over each other in their eagerness to be appointed court-chaplains to King Demos. I am afraid this is what is in many people's minds when they talk of co-operating with the Spirit of the Age. Let the Church strike a bargain with the Labour Party. Let the clergy abuse capitalists and abet strikes from the pulpit. Let them advocate schemes for the forcible redistribution of other people's property. In this way only there is hope of " winning the masses."

Now I am not so unfair as to suppose that no generous and truly Christian motives[1] are mingled with this desire to see the Church plunge into the arena of social strife. The Christian socialist says truly, that so long as the majority of the clergy belong to the upper

---

[1] This sentence was reported: "No generous and Christian motives," &c. This is an extreme, but a typical instance of the way in which my words were handled by the reporters.

and middle classes, they will tend to be imbued with the convictions and prejudices of those classes; and that it is very undesirable that the working-man's point of view should not be recognised by those who labour among them. The sufferings of the poor are often very real, and it is right that Christians should wish to see them relieved. The present distribution of wealth *is* absurd, and, if we believe the Gospels, it must be a greater misfortune for those who have too much than for those who have too little. All that is very true; and I cannot dispute the justice of the remark which Jowett once made, in his detached way: "I am afraid there is more in the Gospels about the danger of being rich and the advantage of being poor, than most of us are willing to admit"; nor even the Bishop of Oxford's words that he had a permanently troubled conscience on the subject, because, while the social position and incomes of the higher clergy place them, and are meant to place them, in the upper, or upper middle class, the Gospel, so far as it takes sides at all, is on the side of the poor and not on the side of the rich.

Nevertheless, I can conceive of nothing more fatal than the policy of enlisting the organised forces of the Church on the side of militant labour. I can recall no instance of a Church which has gone into politics and has not come out badly smirched. Moreover, there are radical and fundamental differences between the view of life taken by social-democracy and the view of Christianity. Put shortly, socialism always assumes that the stye makes the pig, while Christianity declares that the pig makes the stye. Socialism really agrees with the Northern Farmer, that "the poor in a loomp is bad," and that the way to make them good is to see that they " have coats to their backs and take their reg'lar meals." The consistent socialist hates eugenics as much as he hates Christianity, because that science maintains that nature is more important than nurture. Christianity not only maintains but proves triumphantly that the highest life may be led in extreme poverty; though I will state my opinion that we may infer from the teaching of our Lord that He regarded a simple sufficiency—the lot of the well-paid artisan or the small professional man or farmer or tradesman—as the most favourable condition for the higher life. The twelve apostles seem to have belonged to this class. But we can hardly assert too strongly that our Lord set a very low value on the *apparatus* of life. No religion *not* based on harsh asceticism and contempt for civilisation (and Christianity is quite free from this error) ever valued the accessories of life so lightly as the Gospel does. If we take all the Synoptic Gospels together (I admit that St. Luke alone might give a different impression), we shall be struck by the aloofness which our Lord maintained towards economic questions. The refusal to divide the heritage ("Man, who made me a judge or divider over you?") is not to be explained away, especially as we find the story in St. Luke, who, like St. James in the Epistle which bears his name, shows unmistakable traces of the hatred of the rich which was a Jewish tradition. The poor man in the East is always a wronged man, because he cannot afford to buy justice, which is always for sale in those countries. And the Jew is the last man to sit down tamely under such treatment. Sufferance may be the badge of all his tribe; but he never ceases to dream of the pound of flesh, and generally gets it sooner or later. But our Lord's attitude was quite different. He says to the grasping money-grubber not "Thou thief," but "Thou fool." The covetous man is one who is so misguided as "propter vitam vivendi perdere causas." He has assumed that life is only a livelihood. Therefore our Lord reiterates such warnings as, "A man's life consisteth not in the superabundance of the things which he possesseth," "Is not the life more than meat, and the body than raiment?" These are the most characteristic utterances of our Lord about money. Mammon is an exacting master, who will accept no half-hearted service. The American or the English business man knows the truth of that only too well. And God is also an exacting Master, who will accept no half-hearted service. As Huxley once said, with more insight and sympathy than he usually admitted for the religion which he rejected, "It doesn't take much of a man to be a Christian, but it takes all there is of him." Therefore, we must choose whom we will serve. If we choose wrong, we may incidentally inflict superficial injuries upon our neighbours; but it is we ourselves who will suffer most. "So long as thou doest well unto thyself, men will speak good of thee"; and these are the men who, if we believe our Master, are their own worst enemies. Well, the tone of this teaching is quite different from the declamatory praises of voluntary poverty, and rhetorical invectives against avarice, which are sometimes quoted from Ambrose and other Christian Fathers by our Church-socialist friends. This kind of preaching comes not from Christ, but from the Roman rhetorical schools. You will find it at its best or worst in Seneca, "the father of all such as wear shovel hats," as Carlyle unkindly called him; and Seneca, as Nero's prime minister, accumulated a fortune of three millions sterling in a few years, in the intervals of composing these most edifying harangues.

The revolutionary party has long ago made

up its mind about Christianity. "The idea of God must be destroyed," said Marx, the founder of the collectivist theory: "it is the keystone of a perverted civilisation." "The first word of religion is a lie," said his chief lieutenant, Engels. "The revolution denies religion altogether," says Bebel, the leader of the social democratic party in Germany. "Socialism utterly despises the other world," says Mr. Belfort Bax. These men see very clearly that Christianity takes all the sting and fury out of revolutionary agitation. (Of course, it also takes the sting and fury out of the resistance to economic changes; but this they do not think of.) I have good hope that the working-man will not be permanently irreligious and materialistic. At present I think he is no better and no worse than other classes in this respect. We may be sure that many of the handworkers—though not the majority, I fear, of this or any other class—will turn to that Leader who alone can help us, and will take the light yoke and easy burden upon them. But there must be no unholy alliance with a movement which at present is to a large extent based on fundamentally wrong principles. It is treason against our Lord, against His Church, and against the labouring classes themselves, if we secularise our message, and fill our sermons, as some are doing, with echoes of the class-warfare. It is treason to tell them that Christianity has repented of its "otherworldliness," and is now more worthily occupied with parish councils and strikes and free meals and poor-law reform. It is our duty to maintain, in the face of those who nickname the clergy "sky-pilots," that it is otherworldliness which alone has transformed, and can transform, this world.

Otherworldliness, remember, is not belief in a future state of material happiness and misery, in which the inequalities of the present life are to be redressed with interest. It is no invention of the privileged classes, intended to make their less fortunate neighbours content with their lot. That is the mistake of men who can realise no happiness that does not depend on external conditions, and who therefore misunderstand fundamentally the nature of the Christian promise and the foundations of Christian joy. Otherworldliness simply means the conviction of the immeasurable superiority of spiritual goods over material. It maintains that the "transvaluation of all values," which Christ came to establish, is no imaginary thing, but the revelation of actual fact. There are some gains which can only be appropriated at the cost of another's loss. There are some good things which can only be transferred to Peter by robbing Paul. With these Christianity has nothing to do. But there are other good things, of a much higher, more durable, and more satisfying kind, in which one man's gain is not another man's loss; which are unlimited in amount, and indestructible. They belong to the unseen, eternal world, which Christianity maintains to be the real world—the world of which we are citizens. If we once allow this eternal background to drop out of our teaching, we are building on a wrong foundation, and are no longer heralds of the good news which we were ordained to proclaim.

As Christians, we have nothing to do with mankind " in a loomp," whether poor or rich. Let us hear no more of " winning the masses." That is a phrase for politicians, not evangelists. There is not the slightest probability that the largest crowd will ever be gathered in front of the narrow gate. I sometimes think that our absurd superstition about the sanctity of the ballot-box, as an infallible machine for extracting wisdom and truth, has affected our faith. We are actually uncomfortable at being in a minority. Far more wholesome was the state of mind of the statesman who, when his speech was applauded by the mob, said uneasily, " Have I said anything very foolish ? " Christianity always appeals directly to individuals; and its influence radiates out naturally from its focus in the individual soul. That influence is always strongest in the smallest, weakest in the largest circles. *If we ally ourselves with mankind " in the loomp," we shall ally ourselves with mankind at its worst.* It is an unpleasant truth; but one which needs emphasising at present. Bishop Creighton says very truly: "Christianity beautifies many an individual life, and sheds a lustre over many a family. Its influence is less conspicuous in the life of business; it pales in the sphere of what is called society, and is still dimmer in politics; in the region of international obligations it can scarcely be said to exist."[1]

The second temptation of Christ, which, if I am right, symbolises a permanent temptation of His Church, is to trust to miracles, or, as we might perhaps put it, to short cuts, or, remembering the story of the Gordian knot, to cutting knots which should be untied. *The laws of the moral and spiritual life are just as inexorable as those of the physical world.* Nothing worth having is given away; all must be earned. There is no way of dying the death of the righteous except by living the life of the righteous; no way of seeing God except by being pure in heart; no way of believing rightly except by thinking honestly. The lower religions, which are by no means dead ("there are some dead men who have to be killed again in each generation," as a Frenchman said), are mainly fallacious attempts to evade this great law. The whole system of religious magic, with its accompanying demand for "the sacrifice of the in-

[1] *The Heritage of the Spirit,* p. 181.

tellect," is simply this old temptation. "Cast thyself down, for he shall give his angels charge over thee," they tell those who come to them. Laws will be suspended in your favour; we can let you in by private ticket, without much personal trouble. This error is not confined to one school of thought in the Church. It matters little whether cheap forgiveness is offered as the result of the magical efficacy of the Sacraments, or as the result of being " washed in the precious blood of the Lamb." In either case it is false. Spiritual laws are inexorable. Whatsoever a man soweth, that shall he reap—that and nothing else. We are always sowing our future; we are always reaping our past. There is no short cut to the City of God, for men or nations.

The third temptation is, of course, to use questionable means, such as violence and fraud, in the service of the Kingdom of God. It affects our present problem, "The Co-operation of the Church with the Spirit of the Age," in this way. *Our Lord always appealed to men by what was best in them.* Zacchæus craved for human sympathy, and as soon as he found some one who was willing to treat him as a man, and not as a dog, was willing to go through fire and water for him. The poor woman who washed his feet had a loving heart, and could win pardon through her love. It was always the same. Jowett (to quote this half saint, half cynic again) said that "You cannot do anything in managing men without being a bit of a rogue." Jowett's roguery, though it existed, was not of a very shocking kind; but Christ entirely refused to use any policy of this sort. This alone makes it almost impossible for a Christian to mix much in politics, except as one of those impracticable people who can't be bought or bargained with, and who therefore have to be either excluded as hopelessly unpractical, or reckoned with as irreconcilables. When we remember the colossal amount of evil that has been wrought by unscrupulous diplomacy in a good cause, especially by the readiness to take advantage of and utilise the moral defects and weaknesses of others, the vanity of one, the jealousy of another, the avarice of a third—that "knowledge of men" which goes for so much in the art of management—we shall feel the profound significance of this third temptation. There is hardly a single great moral movement which has not been wrecked by getting into the hands of clever, ambitious, unscrupulous schemers. The Church must never "get hold of people," except by their best side. There is a good passage in Mrs. Bosanquet's book, *The Strength of a People*, which I should like to quote in illustration of what I have been saying. "In all considerations of social work and social problems there is one main thing which it is important to remember—that the mind is the man. If we are clear about this great fact, we have an unfailing test to apply to any scheme of social reformation. Does it appeal to men's minds? Not merely to their momentary needs, or appetites, or fancies, but to the higher powers of affection, thought, and reasonable action. The necessity for this appeal has, of course, never been entirely lost sight of. Leaders like Cromwell, who insisted that you could not even make a good soldier out of a man without appealing to his higher qualities, owe their success to their profound knowledge of human nature. Great religious teachers, who have put their faith in spiritual conviction and conversion, who have refused to accept anything short of the whole man, have achieved results which seem miraculous to those who are willing to compromise for a share in the souls they undertake to guide."

Avoiding these snares, what is the Church to do, or rather, what are we humble individual Church people to do, in order to make our faith in Christ an effective force in the social life of our country? Let me put the question in this form, and leave the Spirit of the Age to take care of itself. The deepest Spirit of the Age is on our side; the superficial currents we don't care about, and are certainly not going to float with. How can we best, as Christians, serve our fellow-men?

I am strongly convinced that our whole duty

is this—to hold up the Christian view of life, the Christian standard of values, steadily before the eyes of our generation. To live by that standard ourselves; to show that we are not ashamed of it, that we find that it *works,* that we are ready to defend and justify it to all questioners. It is hardly necessary in this company to enlarge upon the characteristic features of the Christian view of life. We all know the unique stress which our Lord lays on love and sympathy; how He taught us to regard God as a Father to whom we have immediate access at all times and in all places; how He broke down all the barriers, sacred and profane, that separate man from man; how He made everything depend on inwardness—the moral motive of action; how He taught the duty of hopefulness and trust, condemning worry and anxiety; how He taught the necessity of absolute sincerity and single-mindedness; how He advocated plain living without harsh asceticism; how He transformed all values in the light of our divine sonship and heavenly citizenship; how He drew the sting of death by making it the gate of life, and (as part of the same law) showed us how we must die daily to sin, and be reborn unto righteousness. We are to use these convictions of ours in helping to form public opinion, and in setting a standard to others. We may do great good by paying honour where honour is due, and by treating successful rascality with open refusal of respect. We can set an example of simplicity in our way of living, thereby making social amenities easier for the poorer members of our own class, and indirectly for the class below, who are injured, not benefited (as is still often absurdly supposed) by the lavish expenditure of the rich. Nothing is at present more desirable than that the reckless *wastefulness* of our habits—the fault pervades the whole of society from the millionaire to the day-labourer—should be checked. We can set our face against immoral, extravagant, or foolish fashions, reviving some of the wholesome austerity of the old Puritans, Quakers, and Evangelicals; we can try to save what may be saved of the old English Sunday; we can protest vigorously against betting and gambling, including all card-playing for money; and there are many other ways in which we might show that the Church conscience is a real social force, no weaker than the famous "Nonconformist conscience," which is sometimes no more than a rather tortuous and greasy instrument of party politics.[1]

---

[1] Some Nonconformist ministers affected to be very indignant at this sentence, which they construed as a personal insult. I am no enemy to the English and Welsh dissenters; but I think that their habit of mixing religion with politics has almost ruined their spiritual influence in the present generation. There are more ways than one in which "connection with the State" may pervert the energies of a religious body. My words had obviously no reference to Scotland.

These rules of conduct can hardly be called co-operation with the Spirit of the Age. They are rather protests against it. But I think we may find a few modern tendencies which we may, as Church-people, welcome and desire to assist.

The breaking down of class barriers is surely a good thing. Although it is the height of absurdity that every adult male, however foolish or vicious, should have an equal share in governing his neighbours and deciding the policy of the country, it is certainly right that no man should forfeit his citizenship by following a poorly paid calling. And democracy is teaching us, I hope, that there is no reason whatever why a gardener or a bricklayer should not be as good a gentleman as a squire or banker or clergyman. Let us once for all get rid of the snobbish idea that the dignity of our work depends on the kind of work it is, or, worse still, on the scale of our remuneration, instead of on the spirit in which it is performed. Clergymen and teachers are especially in need of remembering this obvious truth. So far is it from being true that the aristocratic ideal (to which I attach great importance) is dependent on class distinctions, that I will boldly maintain that class distinctions ruin that ideal in practice. Those who have studied the social life and habits of the upper classes in the eighteenth century will understand what I mean. Political equality is the caricature of a great truth—that all human beings are *essentially* equal, in this sense, that the moral personality is inviolable. No man or woman is to be merely used, used up, or dishonoured. So far, democracy is reminding us of one of the most original and important parts of the Christian message, and we may "co-operate" without hesitation.

Akin to this is the spread of education. We can never forget that striking passage in which Carlyle compares the untaught masses to a people that had had their right arms maimed. The object of education is to enable every one to make the best of himself. Not necessarily to "better himself"; that ideal could only result in intolerable stress of competition, or an "educated proletariat." When it is once admitted that there are only two claims to respect which can be recognised—character and intellect—(a Platonist would add beauty, perhaps rightly), and that it does not matter a pin what a man's trade is, so long as it is an honest and useful one, a more healthy tone about education will follow. As a Church, we may throw our influence into the scale in favour of sound ideas about education. And if we are as keen about the interests of sound secular education as we ought to be, we shall try to settle the wretched squabble about denominational religious teaching in primary schools in a statesmanlike way, thinking not so much of scoring points for our own denomination as of helping those who want to make our national education efficient and rational.

Thirdly, the care of public health, and the new science of Eugenics, ought surely to have the enthusiastic support of the Church. Progress is only possible if Nature and Nurture are both improved. The betterment of external conditions is the method which produces the quickest results; but these improvements are superficial, precarious, and in part illusory. The real test of progress is the kind of people that a country turns out. No political machinery will work well if the population is of a poor type, physically, mentally, and morally. The elimination of inferior stocks, and the encouragement of the superior to multiply, are absolutely necessary if social degeneration is to be prevented. We have inhibited natural selection; rational selection must take its place.

This gives another reason why the Church should set its face against luxury. Luxury destroys every class or nation that practises it. Nothing fails like success; it kills off families more surely than any oppression that falls short of slavery. A great deal of rabid nonsense has been talked about race-suicide—the births in this country still exceed the deaths by nearly two to one—but the luxurious classes are actually failing to keep up their numbers; and this tendency means that many of the strongest and ablest families are dying out. Edward Carpenter was not far wrong in treating "civilisation" as a racial disease; few races have survived it very long. But now that we know the nature of the malady, and the remedy, we ought to be able to avoid the blunder of sacrificing the higher gains for the lower. Science will soon give us a definite programme of race-hygiene.

These three, I think, are all on right lines. But the main work of the Church must always be to influence the characters of individuals. Listen how St. Augustine apostrophises the Catholic Church:—

"Not only dost thou teach men to worship God with the greatest purity, but thou also teachest them to love their neighbours with a charity which can cure all the evils which sin brings upon human nature. It is thou who bindest wives to their husbands by a chaste and faithful obedience, and husbands to their wives by the laws of sincere love, who makest children subject to their parents by a kind of free servitude, who givest parents a religious authority over their children, who drawest tighter all the bands of nature and of family. Thou makest servants submissive to their masters, masters gentle to their servants. Thou bindest citizens to citizens, nations to nations, in a word, all men to each other, making them not only one society, but one family, by reminding them of their common origin. Thou teachest sovereigns to desire the good of their subjects, subjects to obey their sovereigns; thou prescribest to each of us, to *whom* we owe honour, affection, awe, consolation, advice, exhortation, reproof, punishment; finally, how we ought to be just and charitable towards all."

Does this sound very old-fashioned? Nevertheless, I think St. Augustine was right, and that, as a rule, the duty of the Church is to accept secular institutions and make them work well. We need not be afraid that this will land us in that kind of unprogressive Toryism which stands with both feet firmly stuck in the mud, and says, pompously, "*J' y suis; j' y reste.*" There is no such lever for moving society as religious faith. It *really* moves society, just because it alters the will and character of individuals. There is no political alchemy whereby you can get golden results out of leaden instincts. But make the tree good, and its fruit will also be good. I think we have the highest authority for believing that this is the best, nay, the only true method of social amelioration.

Printed by BALLANTYNE, HANSON & Co.
Edinburgh & London

14 DAY USE
RETURN TO DESK FROM WHICH BORROWED
LOAN DEPT.

This book is due on the last date stamped below, or on the date to which renewed.
Renewed books are subject to immediate recall.

14 Dec '64 L M

NOV 30 '64 - 10 PM

MAR 3 1966 6 5

REC'D LD
APR 16 1966

LD 21A—40m-11,'63
(E1602s10)476B

General Library
University of California
Berkeley

ImTheStory.com

Personalized Classic Books in many genre's

Unique gift for kids, partners, friends, colleagues

Customize:

- Character Names
- Upload your own front/back cover images (optional)
- Inscribe a personal message/dedication on the inside page (optional)

Customize many titles Including
- Alice in Wonderland
- Romeo and Juliet
- The Wizard of Oz
- A Christmas Carol
- Dracula
- Dr. Jekyll & Mr. Hyde
- And more...

Lightning Source UK Ltd.
Milton Keynes UK
UKHW020604030119
334833UK00006B/1096/P